At Home
in the
Mysteries
of Christ: *the grace
of the Rosary*

Jim McManus
C.Ss.R.

Published by **Redemptorist Publications**
Alphonsus House, Chawton, Hampshire, GU34 3HQ, UK
Tel. +44 (0)1420 88222, Fax +44 (0)1420 88805
Email rp@rpbooks.co.uk, www.rpbooks.co.uk

A registered charity limited by guarantee
Registered in England 3261721

Copyright © Redemptorist Publications 2016
First published 2016
Text by Jim McManus C.Ss.R.
Edited by Mandy Woods
Designed by Heather Knight

ISBN 978-0-85231-465-4

A CIP catalogue record for this book is available from the British Library

The publisher gratefully acknowledges permission to use the following copyright
material:

Excerpts from THE JERUSALEM BIBLE, copyright © 1966 by Darton, Longman
& Todd, Ltd and Doubleday, a division of Random House, Inc. Reprinted by
permission.

Cover pictures:
Background - Sayan Puangkham/Shutterstock,
Stained glass window details - JohnArcher/iStock
Rosary - djvstock/Thinkstock

Printed by Lithgo Press Ltd, Leicester LE8 6NU

Other titles by Jim McManus C.Ss.R. available from Redemptorist Publications

The Healing Power of the Sacraments

Healing in the Spirit

Hallowed Be Thy Name

All Generations Will Call Me Blessed

The Inside Job: a spirituality of true self-esteem

I Am My Body: Blessed John Paul's theology of the body

Finding Forgiveness: personal and spiritual perspectives
(with Dr Stephanie Thornton)

Searching for Serenity: spirituality in later life
(with Dr Stephanie Thornton)

Going to Mass: becoming the Eucharist we celebrate

The Fountain of Grace: celebrating 150 years of the Icon of Love

Contents

Preface

My earliest memory of praying as a very young boy was hearing my mother's voice calling our family to attention and saying, "It is time for the Rosary." We all got our Rosary beads, knelt down and recited it, sometimes at great speed, because my older brothers and sisters were keen to get out for the evening.

Many Catholics and, indeed, members of the other Christian Churches are re-discovering today that the Rosary gives us a most effective method for contemplating the mysteries of Christ's life and for personally accepting Christ's invitation when he says, "Make your home in me, as I make mine in you" (John 15:4). For this reason, the title of my book is *At Home in the Mysteries of Christ: the grace of the Rosary.*

As we pray each decade of the Rosary we immerse ourselves in the mystery of Christ's great love for us and we become more aware that the whole work of our salvation is the work of God our Father, carried out by Christ in the power of the Holy Spirit. That is why many see the Rosary as our great Trinitarian prayer.

If you are seeking to revive your own enthusiasm for the Rosary, especially during this Jubilee Year of Mercy, or if you are seeking to learn about the Rosary for the first time, I trust you will find the help and encouragement you need in this book.

I wish to express my sincere thanks to Redemptorist Publications for publishing this book on the Rosary in the Jubilee Year of Mercy. I am also very grateful to Fr Gerard Mulligan, my Rector at St Mary's Monastery in Perth, for his careful proofreading of the manuscript.

Jim McManus C.Ss.R.

Chapter One

At Home in the Mysteries of Christ

The Rosary is the glorious Trinitarian prayer of Catholic spirituality and devotion. It enables us to make our "spiritual home" in the mysteries of Christ. Each decade of the Rosary begins with the prayer Jesus taught us: the *Our Father*. It continues with the contemplation of God in the mysteries of Jesus' life, as we pray the ten *Hail Mary*s, and it concludes with the praise and adoration of the Holy Trinity, as we pray, "Glory be to the Father and to the Son and to the Holy Spirit." The Rosary is a perfect model of Christian contemplative prayer based on the mysteries of Christ, which we contemplate, as Blessed Pope Paul VI said, "through the eyes of her who was closest to the Lord".[1]

The eyes of Mary, as portrayed in the well-known Icon of Our Mother of Perpetual Succour, look straight at us and invite us to enter into the mystery of her Son's life and mission, his death and resurrection. While praying the Rosary in the company of Mary, we enter the mysteries of her Son's life.

As we pray the ten *Hail Mary*s of each decade we contemplate how the mercy of God our Father was revealed to us when Mary consented to become the mother of our Saviour, Jesus Christ. In the words of Pope Francis, "Jesus Christ is the face of the Father's mercy."[2] When we gaze at Jesus, while pondering the mysteries of the Rosary, we behold the mercy of God the Father.

It becomes clear to us that the events of his life and mission on which we meditate and which we call "the mysteries of the Rosary" and "the mysteries of Christ" are all manifestations of the Father's great love for us and the great mercy that he has shown to us.

Blessed Cardinal Newman, speaking to young people at Oscott College in October 1879, said:

> The great power of the Rosary lies in this: that it makes the Creed into a prayer; of course, the Creed is in some sense a prayer and a great act of homage to God; but the Rosary gives us the great truths of His life and death to meditate upon, and brings them nearer to our hearts.[3]

The Rosary provides us with a systematic method for contemplating the mysteries of Christ with our hearts.

Compendium of the Gospel

Many great saints were devotees of the Rosary. In our own time St Pope John Paul II was its great advocate and often spoke of its efficacy in the life of the Church. He wrote:

> The Rosary, though clearly Marian in character, is at heart a Christocentric prayer. In the sobriety of its elements, it has all the *depth of the Gospel message in its entirety*, of which it can be said to be a compendium. It is an echo of the prayer of Mary, her perennial Magnificat for the work of the redemptive Incarnation, which began in her virginal womb.

Twenty mysteries of the Rosary

For many centuries we had the fifteen mysteries of the Rosary: the five Joyful Mysteries, the five Sorrowful Mysteries, and the five Glorious Mysteries. The Joyful Mysteries invited us to meditate on the birth and childhood of Jesus; the Sorrowful Mysteries were a meditation on the Passion and Death of Jesus; and the Glorious Mysteries brought us into the light of the new life of the Resurrection of Jesus. But there was one big, decisive period in the life of Jesus that was not meditated on in those traditional mysteries – namely, that involving Jesus' public ministry of preaching the Gospel. St Pope John Paul II recognised this omission and gave us the Luminous Mysteries, the Mysteries of Light.

The aim of these short reflections on the twenty mysteries of the Rosary is to help you keep the love of the Father, the Son and the Holy Spirit in mind as you say your *Hail Mary*s, moving from contemplating what the Father is doing, in the mysteries of Christ, to contemplating Mary's involvement, through the Holy Spirit, in each of the mysteries of the life, death and resurrection of her Son, Jesus Christ.

Trinitarian structure of the prayer

Each decade of the Rosary begins with the great prayer that Jesus teaches us – the *Our Father*. If, for instance, we are saying the first Joyful Mystery, the Annunciation, we are about to meditate on the mystery of God the Father sending the archangel Gabriel to ask Mary if she would be willing to consent to become the mother of God the Son through the overshadowing of the Holy Spirit. Every mystery of the Rosary – that is, every event in the life and mission of Jesus – comes from the love of God our Father for us human beings. We try to keep this awe-inspiring awareness of the Father's love throughout the whole prayer of the Rosary. That is why we begin each decade of the Rosary with the *Our Father*. We lift our hearts up to the Father in this great prayer. And we conclude each decade by giving glory to the Father, the Son and the Holy Spirit.

Making our home in the mystery

Jesus invites us to make our home in his word and to live by his word. In fact, he says to us, "Make your home in me, as I make mine in you" (John 15:4). Jesus is fond of the word "home". He obviously had a very good "home experience" with his mother Mary and his foster father, St Joseph. He invites us to share and explore the mysteries of his life with him. The Rosary provides us with a systematic way of embarking on this exploration. We explore his home life at Nazareth; we accompany him on his public life of preaching the Gospel; we stay with him throughout the terrors of his passion and death; we exult with him in his glorious resurrection and ascension to heaven. As we make our home in him, in his word, we explore the mysteries of his life and we become united with him in these mysteries. We enter into a deeply personal relationship with Jesus. That personal relationship with Jesus is the very essence of our Christian faith. In the words of Pope Benedict XVI:

> Being a Christian is not the result of an ethical choice or a lofty idea, but the encounter with an event, with a person, which gives life a new horizon and a decisive direction.[4]

It is the very person of Christ whom we encounter as we make our home in the mysteries of the Rosary. While praying the Rosary we are free to move around in this "home of the mysteries" of Christ. Sometimes we are talking to God the Father; at other times we are talking to Mary, the mother of Jesus; throughout the prayer we are absorbing the ethos of the mysteries of Christ: meditating on his love for and obedience to his Father; observing his proclamation of the

Gospel; contemplating him in his great sufferings for us; rejoicing with him in his triumph over death in his resurrection; gratefully receiving from him the gift of the Holy Spirit; and finally, rejoicing with Mary his Mother in her glorious assumption into heaven.

Making our "home" in the mysteries of Christ, and not just "meditating" on the mysteries, as we pray the Rosary, gives us a flexible approach to this great prayer of the Church. For most of us, "meditating on" means "thinking about". While it is good to meditate – to think – about the mysteries, it is also most helpful to consciously say to ourselves that, as we pray each decade of the Rosary, we will make "our home" in the mystery. We will be at "home with Christ".

Making our spiritual home in Christ's word, in his mysteries, fosters a deep Christian spirituality within us:

- a Trinitarian spirituality, acknowledging the Father, the Son and the Holy Spirit;

- a Christocentric spirituality as we contemplate the mysteries of Christ's life, death and resurrection;

- a Marian spirituality, as we seek to see the mysteries of Christ through the eyes of his mother Mary.

In the Rosary we contemplate the face of Christ, but we do so with Mary and through the eyes of Mary. She was the first to experience the mystery of her Son and to ponder that mystery in her heart. We learn from her the secret of "pondering in our hearts", keeping God's word in our hearts, making our "spiritual home" in the mysteries of her Son's life and teaching.

While praying the Rosary we alternate between contemplating the mystery and concentrating on the words. In the *Hail Mary* we are greeting Mary with words the angel used: "Hail, full of grace, the Lord is with you" (Luke 1:28). We can think of the meaning of that greeting in the context of the mystery. We are also saying, in the words of Elizabeth in the Gospel, "Blessed is the fruit of thy womb, Jesus" (Luke 1:42). Again, as we think about Jesus, the fruit of Mary's womb, in the light of the mystery, our mind and spirit can be lifted up to God in new ways. On the other hand, we may be quite unaware of the words we are saying as we concentrate on the mystery. As we focus, for instance, on the crucifixion or the resurrection of Jesus, the words can become just a rhythmic melody in the background of our awareness while our whole attention is taken up with the Lord, either in his great suffering or in his glorious triumph over death.

Coping with distractions

The essence of our prayer is not in the perfect *performance* but in the loving *intention* to give the time to God. When we enter into his presence in our prayer time, God sees the *intention* in our hearts. God knows we want to spend this time with him. When we say to ourselves or a few friends, "Let's say our Rosary," God accepts that good intention and even if our thoughts wander far away from the mysteries of Christ, our intention to pray the Rosary remains in place. It is our intention, and not our wandering thoughts, that God sees and accepts.

The fact that our minds wander – that our thoughts are so often about other things – doesn't mean that we have left God's presence. We are not our thoughts. We remain where our hearts want to be, and right now our hearts want to be with God in prayer. Our thoughts don't change the desire of our hearts. As we pray the mysteries of the Rosary we want to make "our home" in the mysteries of Christ. That is what our hearts want. But our thoughts will certainly wander during this prayer. These involuntary distractions, this wandering of our minds – these things do not undermine our prayer.

A loving, contemplative glance

Each time, as we become aware of these distractions, we gently refocus, bring our minds back to where we are in the mysteries of Christ, and continue peacefully with our prayer. The moment you become aware that your thoughts are elsewhere, that is a moment of grace. The Holy Spirit is reminding you that you can now take a loving, contemplative glance at the mystery of the Rosary that you are praying. For instance, if you become aware that you have been totally distracted while praying the first joyful mystery, the Annunciation, you now have the grace to take a loving glance at Mary saying her "Yes" to God as she says, "Let it be done unto me according to your word." Or, if you have almost finished the third glorious mystery, the Descent of the Holy Spirit, with your thoughts far removed from the divine, you can now gaze afresh at that great gift of the Holy Spirit given to the first disciples and now given to us.

We can turn our very distractions into moments of real contemplation. It is our thoughts, and not the desire in our hearts for our time with God, that are easily distracted. Our hearts remain where we want to be. In our time of prayer we want to be with God, at home with Christ. We never allow the distractions to convince us that we cannot pray or that we are wasting our time trying to pray. We are always reassured by the words of St Paul: "The Spirit comes to help us in our weakness, for, when we do not know how to pray properly, then the Spirit personally makes our petitions for us in groans that cannot be put into words; and he who can see into all hearts knows what the Spirit means because the prayers that the Spirit makes for God's holy people are always in accordance with the mind of God" (Romans 8:26–27).

The Rosary, despite all our distractions, leads us into the contemplation of the mysteries of our faith, because, in spending time with Mary, in seeing the mysteries of Christ through her eyes, we begin to assimilate her spirit and we begin to see Christ as she sees him.

We are not obliged to say the Rosary, but of all the methods of prayer that have been discovered and developed in the Church throughout the centuries, there is none more effective or more enriching than the Rosary.

Our Mother of Perpetual Succour

In saying the Rosary, we are spending time with Mary, whom the Church calls "Our Mother of Perpetual Succour" or "Our Mother of Perpetual Help". Mary has many inspiring titles in our Catholic tradition. But for many of us, the most comforting and reassuring title is "Mother of Perpetual Succour". In our weakness, in the midst of our failures and disappointments in life, we all cry out for a mother's love and help. Mary is always at hand to offer us the help we need. There is no better way to approach Mary for her motherly help than to contemplate the face of Jesus her Son, the face of God the Father's mercy. Mary herself contemplated the mystery of the Father's mercy when she conceived the Son of God in her womb. She was the herald of this mercy to her cousin Elizabeth. Elizabeth, filled with the Holy Spirit, cried out, "Of all women you are the most blessed, and blessed is the fruit of your womb. Why should I be honoured with a visit from the mother of my Lord? For the moment your greeting reached my ears, the child in my womb leapt for joy. Yes, blessed is she who believed that the promise made to her by the Lord would be fulfilled" (Luke 1:42–45). Mary responds to Elizabeth with her wonderful *Magnificat* in which she explains what is going on inside her with these words:

> "His mercy reaches from age to age for those who fear him... He has come to the help of Israel his servant,

mindful of his mercy... of his mercy to Abraham and to his descendants for ever" (Luke 1:50,54–55).

Mary understands her pregnancy, the mystery of the Son of God becoming incarnate in her womb, as the act in which God remembers his mercy.

Different ways of praying the Rosary

We have a great variety of ways of praying the Rosary. Some say a single Rosary – that is, the five decades – each day, while others may say several. Some recite it while out walking or driving, while others find a quiet place in their home or in a church. Some belong to a dedicated group which meets regularly to pray the Rosary as a community of faith. Again, some devotees say just one decade each day and take their time to make their home in the mystery they are contemplating. Whatever your preference, it is always helpful to try and take a fresh look at each mystery.

In these short reflections on the twenty mysteries of the Rosary I try to look at each mystery from different points of view. Each has profound meaning for our own lives. My hope is that these reflections will help you make the connection between the mystery of Christ and the mystery of your own life.

Christ invites us to make our home in these mysteries. We need a great grace to accept his invitation because we are often so preoccupied with other things. That is why I conclude each reflection with this simple prayer of petition to Our Mother of Perpetual Succour:

O Mother of Perpetual Succour, obtain for us the grace to make our home in this Mystery of your Son, our Lord Jesus Christ, as we meditate on the great mercy that the "Father of mercies" has shown to us.

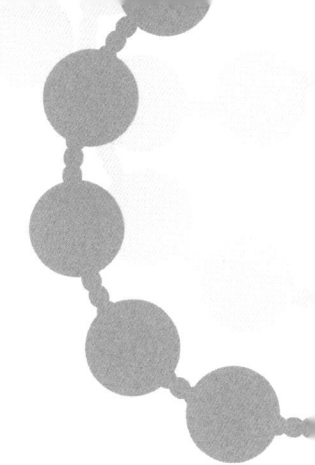

Chapter Two

The Joyful Mysteries

The First Joyful Mystery

The Annunciation

God the Father had promised that he would save us from our sins, restore us to his friendship, and bring us into a new covenant of love with himself (Jeremiah 31:31). As we pray this first decade of the Rosary we are gazing at how God the Father begins to fulfil his promise. He sends his archangel Gabriel to ask the Virgin Mary to become the mother of his Son through whom he will fulfil his promise. Mary asked the archangel how such a motherhood could come about since she was a virgin and Gabriel told her that "the Holy Spirit will come upon you and the power of the Most High will cover you with its shadow. And so the child will be holy and will be called Son of God" (Luke 1:35). When Mary heard Gabriel's answer to her question she believed and said, "I am the handmaid of the Lord, let what you have said be done to me" (Luke 1:38).

Willing Collaborator in God's Plan

In this first mystery of the Rosary we meet "the Father of mercies" (2 Corinthians 1:3) revealing to the young Virgin Mary his plan for our "divinisation". God the Son will become human so that by sharing in our humanity we can share in his divinity. Mary consented to God's request. She became the mother of our Saviour, the Son of God. She became the willing collaborator in God's great plan for our salvation. When God the Father asked Mary, through the angel, to be the mother of his Son he greeted her with the first words of our *Hail Mary*: "Hail, full of grace, the Lord is with you". God invites Mary into the closest collaboration imaginable. She will give birth to the Son of God and mother him from the cradle to the grave. In willingly collaborating with God's plan for our salvation, for our "divinisation", Mary makes it possible for us to become sons and daughters of God.

While we are saying the *Our Father* we can linger on those words, "our Father". We want to become more aware of the depth of the Father's mercy and love. But we are also contemplating the love of the Virgin Mary, who, by consenting to become the mother of the Son of God, makes possible the fulfilment of God's plan for our salvation.

Journeying with Mary

We begin a long journey with Mary as we say the *Hail Mary*s in this first decade. She has received from God the vocation to be the mother of Jesus, to bring our holy Redeemer into the world. We can sit with her in silent contemplation as she says in her heart, "He has looked on his lowly servant" and, "The Lord has done great things for me" (Luke 1:49). As we sit with her in prayer, in this mystery, we remember that at that moment, in the history of our salvation, Mary was the only person in the whole world who believed in the mystery of her Son Jesus: the mystery that the Son of God had become incarnate in her womb.

Mary has become the collaborator with God the Father in the fulfilment of his plan for our salvation. She now carries within her womb the Son of God, who has become her own son. The rest of her life will be defined by this great moment in the history of our salvation. Mary of Nazareth has become Mary the mother of Jesus the Son of God and will become, through the word of Jesus from the cross, Mary the Mother of the Church of Christ, the mother of each of us.

Woman of Faith: the first Christian disciple

We sit with Mary, saying our ten *Hail Marys*, contemplating the mystery that she herself is now living, the mystery of God the Father's choice of her and the great grace he gave her as the Holy Spirit overshadowed her and Jesus was conceived in her womb. The Father has entrusted his Son to Mary and we too are likewise invited to entrust ourselves to her. We allow ourselves to be drawn into the mystery we are contemplating. We make our home in the mystery. We may not be able to put any aspect of this mystery into words; we may not be able to keep our minds focused because our thoughts fly all over the place; but we are praying in a way that gives God glory and honour. And so we conclude our decade with the great prayer of praise: *Glory be to the Father and to the Son and to the Holy Spirit.* We return in praise and thanksgiving to the great mystery of the Holy Trinity.

Prayer of Intercession

O Mother of Perpetual Succour, obtain for us the grace to make our home in this Mystery of your Son, our Lord Jesus Christ, as we meditate on the great mercy that the "Father of mercies" has shown to us.

The Second Joyful Mystery
The Visitation

When Mary consented to God's invitation to become the mother of Jesus she identified herself as "the handmaid of the Lord" (Luke 1: 38). Now, the Lord is sending her on a missionary journey of love and support for her elderly cousin. The archangel Gabriel told her that Elizabeth "has, in her old age, conceived a son, and she whom people called barren is now in her sixth month, *for nothing is impossible to God*" (Luke 1:37). Mary believed what Gabriel said about Elizabeth being in her sixth month and left immediately to make the long journey from Nazareth "to a town in the hill country of Judah. She went into Zechariah's house and greeted Elizabeth" (Luke 1:39–40).

John the Baptist Leaps for Joy in His Mother's Womb

God the Father wanted Mary to go, carrying the promised redeemer in her womb, to be with her cousin Elizabeth, who would soon give birth to her son, the great John the Baptist. God the Father was present as these two chosen women met and greeted each other. St Luke described what happened with these words:

> Now as soon as Elizabeth heard Mary's greeting, the child leapt in her womb and Elizabeth was filled with the Holy Spirit. She gave a loud cry and said: "Of all women you are the most blessed, and blessed is the fruit of your womb. Why should I be honoured with a visit from the mother of my Lord? For the moment your greeting reached my ears, the child in my womb leapt for joy. Yes, blessed is she who believed that the promise made her by the Lord would be fulfilled. (Luke 1:41–45)

In response, Mary proclaimed God's great mercy:

My soul proclaims the greatness of the Lord
and my spirit *exults in God my Saviour;*
because *he has looked upon his lowly handmaid.*
Yes, from this day forward all generations will call me
blessed,
for the Almighty has done great things for me.
Holy is his name,
and *his mercy reaches from age to age for those who fear
him.*
He has shown the power of his arm,
he has routed the proud of heart.
He has pulled down princes from their thrones *and
exalted the lowly.*
The hungry he has filled with good things, the rich sent
empty away.
*He has come to the help of Israel his servant, mindful of
his mercy*
—according to the promise made to our ancestors—
of his mercy to Abraham and to his descendants for ever.
(Luke 1:46–55).

Mary proclaims to Elizabeth and to us that the mystery of her
pregnancy, the mystery of the Incarnation of the Son of God in her
womb, is the act by which God "remembers his mercy". She invites
us to ponder with her the great mercy of God that has now become
incarnate in her womb.

The Holy Spirit is Poured Out

In the meeting of these two holy women we are witnessing God
the Father pouring out the Holy Spirit on Elizabeth and sanctifying
her son, John the Baptist, in her womb. Notice that it is the very
voice of Mary that the Father uses to impart such a great blessing.

Elizabeth said, "For the moment your greeting reached my ears the child in my womb leapt for joy." Mary's very presence, her very voice, becomes, as it were, a sacrament for the outpouring of the Holy Spirit. And not just on Elizabeth and the baby in her womb. Zechariah, who had been struck dumb because he didn't believe the archangel Gabriel's word about his wife Elizabeth bearing him a son in her old age, also received the gift of the Spirit. When his son is born, he names him John, as the archangel told him, and he too "was filled with the Holy Spirit and spoke this prophecy: '*Blessed be the Lord, the God of Israel*, for he has visited his people, he has come to their rescue'" (Luke 1:67–68).

Mary's presence in the house of Zechariah, like the presence of the Ark of the Covenant in the household of Obed-edom (2 Samuel 6:12), brings great blessings from the Lord. The Church honours Mary with the title *Ark of the Covenant* in the Litany of Loreto. Wherever Mary is welcomed, as she was welcomed by Elizabeth, the Holy Spirit becomes present and active.

The Gift of Faith

As we pray this decade of the Rosary we accompany Mary on her journey from Nazareth to the hill country of Judah. Mary is doing God's will and becoming the bearer of God's mercy to Elizabeth's household. At Mary's greeting, Elizabeth is filled with faith by the Holy Spirit and cries out, "Why should I be honoured with a visit from the mother of my Lord?" (Luke 1:43). Elizabeth believes that the child in Mary's womb is her Lord. And Zechariah is given that same faith when he says in prophecy about his own son, "You, little child, you shall be called Prophet of the Most High, for you will go before the Lord to prepare the way for him" (Luke 1:76). Elizabeth is the first to believe that Mary is the mother of the Lord, and then her husband Zechariah receives that same faith and proclaims that his son will "prepare the way of the Lord" whom he calls "the tender mercy of our God" (Luke 1:78).

"Making our home" in this mystery of the Visitation enables us to walk with Mary on her journey of faith and receive through her presence in our lives the blessings that Elizabeth and Zechariah received from Mary's presence in their household. Mary is very close to us when we pray the Rosary. She hears our prayer; she is delighted with our prayers for others. She is Our Mother of Perpetual Succour and when we pray for others she will always respond.

The prayer that is most pleasing to Our Lady is the beautiful prayer of praise with which we conclude each decade of her Rosary. She joins us, with the whole court of heaven, when we say, "Glory be to the Father and to the Son and to the Holy Spirit." Even if you are very distracted as you pray the decades of the Rosary, try to recollect yourself and invite Our Lady to join you as you pray this great prayer of praise.

Prayer of Intercession

O Mother of Perpetual Succour, obtain for us the grace to make our home in this Mystery of your Son, our Lord Jesus Christ, as we meditate on the great mercy that the "Father of mercies" has shown to us.

The Third Joyful Mystery
The Birth of Jesus

God the Father's plan for our salvation involved not just the remission of our sins, but God the Son becoming a human being, sharing in our very humanity, so that we could share in his divinity and truly become sons and daughters of God. St Paul said, "For anyone who is in Christ, there is a new creation; the old order is gone and a new being is there to see" (2 Corinthians 5:17). The Virgin Mary willingly collaborated with the Father's plan of redemption. Through the power of the Holy Spirit she became the mother of the Son of God. Now the moment has arrived and Mary gives birth to Jesus, her son who is also the divine Son of God.

Joy in Heaven

There is joy in heaven at the birth of Jesus. The angel of the Lord appeared to the shepherds in the fields of Bethlehem saying, "Do not be afraid. Listen, I bring you news of great joy, a joy to be shared by all the people" (Luke 2:10). In praying this mystery of the Rosary we open our hearts to this joy. We want to celebrate with the angels, with the shepherds, but most of all with God, the Father of Jesus, and with Mary, his mother. Joy, St Paul tells us, is the "fruit of the Holy Spirit" (Galatians 5:22).

True God and True Man

We are about to meditate on the most amazing truth of God's relationship with us human beings. God, who is the creator of the whole universe, including mankind, has now become a created human being and is born into human history as the child of Mary. Like each of us, Jesus can say to God the Father, "It was you who knit me together in my mother's womb" (Psalm 139:13). God the Son didn't just appear to be born as a man. That was a very ancient heresy known as Docetism. It claimed that Jesus was a divine being who only took on human appearance but not human flesh. Jesus is truly human, truly the son of Mary, sharing truly in our humanity, while remaining, at the same time, the infinite Son of God.

In meditating on this mystery of the Rosary we begin as usual by saying the *Our Father*. As we say, "Hallowed be thy name" we could pause for a moment and gaze at how God is indeed making his name holy in our very humanity, in the infant Jesus, his Son, who is born as our brother in that stable in Bethlehem. Jesus is truly the new creation. As the Church prays in the Preface of the Mass for Christmas, "In the mystery of the Word made flesh, a new light of your glory has shone upon the eyes of our mind, so that, as we recognise in him God made visible, we may be caught up, through him, in love of things invisible." It is the Father's glory that we see shine in the birth of Jesus. We see the Father hallowing his name on earth. Could the Father have shown any greater love for us than is now embodied in the flesh and blood of the infant Jesus who is born as our brother?

Mary's Joy

Our thoughts and affections, of course, are with Mary, who has given birth to her son, Jesus. Like any young mother, she is filled with immense joy as she beholds for the first time the face of her newborn son. She had explained to her cousin Elizabeth that her pregnancy, the incarnation of the Son of God in her womb, was the act in which "God was remembering his mercy". Now, as she gazes for the first time on her son, she sees "the face of the Father's mercy". As Pope Francis says:

> Jesus Christ is the face of the Father's mercy. These words might well sum up the mystery of the Christian faith. Mercy has become living and visible in Jesus of Nazareth, reaching its culmination in him.[5]

Mary now holds in her arms and suckles at her breasts the "mercy of God incarnate" in her own son, Jesus. She is truly the *Mother of Mercy*.

Joseph, her husband, the foster father of Jesus, was with Mary to share her joy. It was he who brought Mary on the journey from

Nazareth to Bethlehem so that the child would be born where the prophet had foretold (Matthew 2:5).

Visitors to the home of a newborn child often say, "Isn't he adorable?" In the case of the baby Jesus, the word *adorable* accurately describes the feelings and the reverence that are in our hearts as we gaze on the holy infant, "the face of the Father's mercy". Before too long, as the Gospel recounts, the Wise Men arrived, "and going into the house, they saw the child and his mother Mary, and falling to their knees they did him homage" (Matthew 2:11). As we pray this decade of the Rosary we too "fall to our knees" as we see "the child and his mother" and we adore the infinite love and mercy of God the Father made visible to us through his Son, born as our brother and our Saviour. When we say our *Hail Mary*s we may want to emphasise in our minds and hearts the truth of what we say when we pray, "Holy Mary, mother of God." The infant that she holds on her knees is truly God.

We conclude this decade with the wonderful prayer, the *Glory be to the Father*. We remind ourselves that the three divine persons, Father, Son and Holy Spirit, are intimately involved in the mystery on which we are meditating. It is the Father who sent his Son to become the saviour of humankind by becoming a human being like us. And it was through the Holy Spirit overshadowing the Virgin Mary that the Son of God became incarnate in her womb and was born into this world as Jesus, son of Mary and our brother.

Prayer of Intercession

O Mother of Perpetual Succour, obtain for us the grace to make our home in this Mystery of your Son, our Lord Jesus Christ, as we meditate on the great mercy that the "Father of mercies" has shown to us.

The Fourth Joyful Mystery

The Presentation of the Child Jesus in the Temple

The Law of Moses required that "every first born male must be consecrated to the Lord" (Luke 2:23). In accordance with this law, the parents of Jesus brought him to the Temple to offer him to the Lord. They entered the Temple as a poor couple, to offer their son to God and to make the offering of the poor, *"a pair of turtle doves or two young pigeons"* (Luke 2:24). Other poor couples there that day probably made the very same offering.

The entrance of Jesus into the Temple of God his Father was revealed by the Holy Spirit to those who were waiting in hope for the coming of the redeemer of God's people. The Holy Spirit had revealed to Simeon, who "looked forward to Israel's comforting", that he would not die "until he had set eyes on the Christ of the Lord" (Luke 2:26). Simeon is led by the Spirit to the Temple and is there to take the Child Jesus in his arms and give praise to God. Enlightened by the Holy Spirit, Simeon saw in Mary's child the promised redeemer.

He also saw that the "price" her son would pay for our redemption would cause Mary great inner pain. He said to her, "You see this child: he is destined for the fall and the rising of many in Israel, destined to be a sign that is rejected – and a sword will pierce your own soul too – so that the secret thoughts of many may be laid bare" Luke 2:34–35). While Simeon was still speaking to Mary and Joseph, Anna, a prophetess, "came by just at that moment and began to praise God; and she spoke of the child to all who looked forward to the deliverance of Jerusalem" (Luke 2:38). Simeon and Anna, like Elizabeth and Zechariah, are the faithful Israelites who have been living in hope as they waited for the coming of the Messiah. They were there to welcome him when he came to the Temple.

The Perfect Offering

In meditating on this mystery we accompany Mary and Joseph on their journey to the Temple to present the child Jesus to the Lord. No human couple could ever make the perfect offering that Mary and Joseph are now about to make to God the Father: the Child Jesus, the divine Son of God whom the Father has sent into the world as our Saviour.

Boundless Mercy

God the Father's mercy has no bounds. The Father loves us as he loves Jesus, and when he sees us, he sees Jesus. We open our hearts as we pray this decade of the Rosary, to share in God the Father's joy as Mary and Joseph present the Baby Jesus in the Temple.

While we pray the *Our Father* at the beginning of this decade, we take a moment to allow the words "Our Father" to enter more deeply into our hearts. The Father of Jesus Christ is also our Father. It is Jesus himself who teaches us to call God "our Father". Through praying the Rosary, our relationship with God deepens, becomes more intimate and personal, more trusting and grateful. The words of the Mass begin to echo in our hearts: "You are all holy, O Lord, and all you have created rightly gives you praise, for through your Son, our Lord Jesus Christ, by the power and working of the Holy Spirit, you give life to all things and make them holy and you never cease to gather a people to yourself, so that from the rising of the sun to its setting, a pure sacrifice may be offered to your name."[6] In presenting the Child Jesus in the Temple, Mary and Joseph are offering a pure sacrifice.

Pondering in Her Heart

While saying our *Hail Mary*s we stand with Mary as she offers her child to God, increasingly aware that the salvation which Jesus would bring to his people would come at a great price. She would ponder Simeon's words about her child being "destined to be a sign that is rejected" and about the sword that will pierce her own soul. As St Luke said, "His mother kept all these things in her heart" (Luke 2:51). She would meditate on them and grow in her understanding of the mission and destiny of her son. Again she would say "Yes" to the Father. She would pray "thy will be done on earth as it is in heaven". She would teach Jesus, as a small boy, to pray to God in that same way!

"Making our home" in this mystery opens our eyes to the central role that Mary plays in the work of our salvation. At God's request, she consented to become the mother of the Son and now she consents to make a total offering of her son Jesus to the Father. While remaining her beloved child, he is now totally consecrated to the Father and will put the Father's will before her wishes or desires. We admire Mary's faith, her total trust in God and her unconditional surrender to his will. Throughout her life she prayed, "Let it be done to me according to thy word" (Luke 1:38).

The Holy Spirit alerted Simeon and Anna to the fact that the long-awaited time had come and that the promised Messiah was being carried into the Temple in his mother's arms. With great gratitude, we can echo their words of prophecy and praise as we conclude our decade with *Glory be to the Father and to the Son and to the Holy Spirit.*

Prayer of Intercession

O Mother of Perpetual Succour, obtain for us the grace to make our home in this Mystery of your Son, our Lord Jesus Christ, as we meditate on the great mercy that the "Father of mercies" has shown to us.

The Fifth Joyful Mystery
The Finding in the Temple

In our meditation on this mystery we join Mary and Joseph with the twelve-year-old Jesus and the rest of the "the pilgrim community" of Nazareth as they make their annual pilgrimage to the Temple in Jerusalem for the feast of the Passover. Having fulfilled all their religious duties, they had travelled for a day back north towards Nazareth, when Mary and Joseph realised that Jesus, whom they had supposed to be with his relatives and boys of his own age, was not among them. We can easily imagine their fears and anxieties as they retraced their steps to Jerusalem "looking for him everywhere" along the road.

Different Emotions

On the third day they found him in the Temple. He was just a boy of twelve, yet he was "sitting among the doctors, listening to them and asking them questions; and all those who heard him were astounded at his intelligence and his replies" (Luke 2:47). But his parents responded quite differently. St Luke describes it thus: "They were overcome when they saw him, and his mother said to him, 'My child, why have you done this to us? See how worried your father and I have been, looking for you.' Jesus said to them, 'Why were you looking for me? Did you not know that I must be busy with my Father's affairs?'" (Luke 2:48–49). Mary and Joseph "did not understand what he meant" (Luke 2:50).

Jesus was, in effect, saying to his mother, "I must do what my Father wants me to do." As Pope Benedict XVI pointed out:

> Mary had said: "Your father and I have been looking for you anxiously." Jesus corrects her: I am with my father. My father is not Joseph, but another – God himself. It is to him

that I belong, and here I am with him. Could Jesus' divine sonship be presented any more clearly?[7]

Mary Ponders in Her Heart

St Luke concludes this painful episode for Mary and the twelve-year-old Jesus with the words, "He then went down with them and came to Nazareth and lived under their authority. His mother stored up all these things in her heart. And Jesus increased in wisdom, in stature, and in favour with God and men" (Luke 2:51–52).

Mary also increased in wisdom as she "stored up" in her heart what Jesus had said. Sometimes we might think that because Mary knew that Jesus had been conceived by the Holy Spirit, she understood everything about his mission and destiny. But Mary had to live her life and motherhood by faith, not by understanding. As Elizabeth said to her, "Blessed is she who believed" (Luke 1:45). By "pondering in her heart" what Jesus said, by accepting his word, even though she found it difficult to understand, Mary grew in the faith that eventually gave her the courage to stand at the foot of the cross. Unlike us, Mary was sinless, and as she pondered the words of Jesus in her heart, she grew in her understanding and total acceptance of his mission and destiny.

God the Father had great compassion for Mary and Joseph as they experienced the loss of their son and searched anxiously for him. He knew that although they couldn't understand what was happening to them at that time, they would understand later.

The Father has that same compassion and care for us when we find ourselves faced with problems we cannot understand and which we cannot resolve.

St Peter encourages us with these words: *"Unload all your worries on to the Lord, since he is looking after you"* (1 Peter 5:7). The Father who looked after Mary and Joseph during those three days when they were searching for Jesus is also looking after us. If we hand over our worries to the Lord, we will experience his loving care. God the Father is with us in every situation, no matter how frightening or hopeless it may seem. God has reassured us with these words: "Does a woman forget her baby at the breast, or fail to cherish the son of her womb? Yet even if these forget, I will never forget you" (Isaiah 49:15).

Searching with Mary

As we say our *Hail Marys* we can easily empathise with Mary and Joseph as they anxiously search for their child. We have all experienced loss. Their son Jesus was missing for three days. They had searched anxiously for him. Then they found him. St Luke is also teaching us a deeper lesson here about our relationship with God. Sometimes we find ourselves in a time of darkness when we have lost what we have greatly treasured. It is then that we need to join Mary in her search for Jesus.

Anxiety and worry are the appropriate emotions in a mother who loses her child and can't find him. We shouldn't be afraid of those same emotions when we are facing some loss or trouble in our own life. As we join Mary in her search for Jesus, she will teach us how to remain in God's presence as we "anxiously search everywhere" for the solution to our problems. She is always with us as Our Mother of Perpetual Succour.

St Paul says, "Be happy at all times; pray constantly; and for all things give thanks to God, because this is what God expects you to do in Christ Jesus" (1 Thessalonians, 5:17). We give thanks to God for all things, for all our losses, for all our troubles, as we conclude our meditation on this mystery of the Rosary by saying with our whole heart, *Glory be to the Father and to the Son and to the Holy Spirit.*

Prayer of Intercession

O Mother of Perpetual Succour, obtain for us the grace to make our home in this Mystery of your Son, our Lord Jesus Christ, as we meditate on the great mercy that the "Father of mercies" has shown to us.

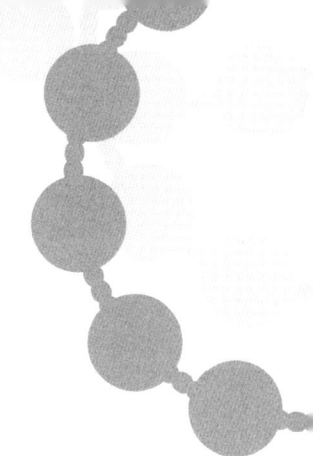

Chapter Three

The Mysteries of Light

The First Mystery of Light

Jesus is Baptised by John the Baptist in the Jordan

In praying the Rosary we first met John the Baptist when his mother was visited by Our Blessed Lady. During that visit his mother Elizabeth said to Mary, "The moment your greeting reached my ears, the child in my womb leapt for joy" (Luke 1:44). Thirty years later that child has grown into the great prophet John the Baptist and is, as his father Zechariah had prophesied, "going before the Lord to prepare the way for him" (Luke 1:76). John, full of the Holy Spirit, has been preaching a baptism of repentance. Great crowds are going to receive this baptism and change their lives. Jesus also went to John.

The Baptist Witnesses to Jesus

When the Baptist first saw Jesus approaching he said to his disciples, "There is the lamb of God who takes away the sin of the world. This is the one I spoke of when I said: A man is coming after me who ranks before me because he existed before me" (John 1:29–30). The Baptist told his own disciples, "You yourselves can bear me out: I said, I am not the Christ; I am the one who has been sent in front of him. The bride is only for the bridegroom; and yet the bridegroom's friend, who stands there and listens, is glad when he hears the bridegroom's voice" (John 3:28–29). John the Baptist called Jesus the "lamb of God" and the "bridegroom". He believed that Jesus "is the Chosen One of God" (John 1:34). We can understand, therefore, that when Jesus presented himself to John for baptism, the Baptist hesitated and said, "I should be baptised by you and do you come to me?" (Matthew 3:14). The Baptist knew that Jesus didn't need his baptism of repentance. But what he didn't fully realise was that Jesus, in seeking this baptism, was identifying himself completely with sinners. As Pope Benedict XVI explained:

> Jesus loaded the burdens of mankind's guilt upon his shoulders; he bore it down into the depths of the Jordan. He inaugurated his public activity by stepping into the place of sinners. His inaugural gesture is an anticipation of the cross.[8]

Jesus Takes Our Place

Jesus, in his baptism by John, now stands before God totally identified with all sinners, whose sins he came to take away. As Jesus came up out of the water and was at prayer, "heaven opened and the Spirit of God came down and rested upon him like a dove and a voice came from heaven, you are my beloved Son in whom I am well pleased" (Luke 3:21–22). God the Father is pleased with Jesus, his Son, who has totally identified himself with fallen humanity, and he pours out afresh on him the presence and blessing of the Holy Spirit. Notice that it was while "Jesus was at prayer", and not through John's baptism, that the Father poured out the promised Spirit.

It is through the Holy Spirit that Jesus now begins his public ministry of preaching the Gospel. First of all, St Luke tells us, "Jesus was led by the Spirit into the desert", where he prayed and fasted for forty days and was tempted by the devil. Having overcome all the temptations of the devil, St Luke tells us, "Jesus, with the power of the Spirit in him, returned to Galilee" (Luke 4:14). Now he begins his work of preaching the Gospel.

Our meditation on this mystery of the baptism of Jesus will help us to deepen our awareness that the whole ministry of Jesus is the work of God the "Father of mercies" (2 Corinthians 1:3). As Jesus himself said, "It is the Father, living in me, who is doing this work" (John 14:10).

God the Father Reveals the True Identity of Jesus

As we "make our home" in this mystery we become aware that it is the Father who is manifesting the true identity of Jesus as he pours out the Holy Spirit upon him and says to him, "You are my Son, the Beloved; my favour rests on you" (Luke 3:22). In his beloved Son's baptism, the Father sees him totally identified with our sinful human nature. He is well pleased with what he sees. Jesus, who is, in the words of the Baptist, "the bridegroom", will bring all the sins of God's people, who are "his bride", to the cross and restore us to our full dignity as sons and daughters of God, our Father. As St Peter said, we are now "able to share the divine nature" (2 Peter 1:4).

Mary, of course, knew that the time had come for Jesus to leave their home. She had looked after him for thirty years. Now he must begin doing the work that God had sent him to do. She had been there when John the Baptist was born and she had heard his father Zechariah prophesy that John "would go before the Lord to prepare a way for him". When she heard what John was doing down at the river Jordan, she would have known that the time had come for Jesus to leave home. Yet, like any mother whose only son is now leaving home, Mary surely felt the pain of separation. Her deep faith sustained her as she lived her prayer of consent, "I am the handmaid of the Lord, let what you have said be done to me" (Luke 1:38). Indeed, wherever Jesus went, Mary went with him because Mary was the first "to make her home in him" (John 15:4).

While we say our *Hail Marys* we remain close to Mary, as all her thoughts would have been with Jesus, who had gone to John the Baptist. Mary knew the prophecies. She had received one very directly from Simeon when he spoke about her Son being a "sign of contradiction" and of the "sword" that would pierce her own soul. She is now at one with Jesus as he leaves their home to do what the Father sent him to do, to redeem his brothers and sisters. She will be there for him at every critical moment. When the hour of his death on the cross comes, she will be there. During these three years of Jesus' public ministry of preaching the Gospel, Mary will become increasingly identified with the mission of her Son.

Jesus and the Spirit

At the baptism of Jesus, the Holy Spirit began to lead and empower Jesus in all that he did. But Jesus didn't just receive the Holy Spirit for himself. He received the Spirit for us. He said to his disciples, "You will receive the power of the Holy Spirit which will come to you, and then you will be my witnesses" (Acts 1:8). We "make our home" in this mystery and rejoice at the coming of the Spirit on Jesus at his baptism. We open our hearts in this mystery to receive that same Spirit which Jesus wants to give to us afresh each day. As we conclude this decade we keep the Spirit's role especially in mind while saying, *Glory be to the Father and to the Son and to the Holy Spirit.*

Prayer of Intercession

O Mother of Perpetual Succour, obtain for us the grace to make our home in this Mystery of your Son, our Lord Jesus Christ, as we meditate on the great mercy that the "Father of mercies" has shown to us.

The Second Mystery of Light

The Wedding Feast in Cana

St John could have introduced the public ministry of Jesus by recounting some of his great teachings, or his healing miracles, or his arguments with the Scribes and Pharisees. He chose, however, to begin his account of Jesus' Gospel preaching with the story of a wedding feast. We read, "On the third day there was a wedding feast in Cana in Galilee. The mother of Jesus was there, and Jesus and his disciples had also been invited" (John 2:1–2).

The provision of wine for the wedding feast was the responsibility of the bridegroom. At this wedding in Cana something had gone badly wrong. We are told, "When the wine ran out, since the wine provided for the wedding was all finished, the mother of Jesus said to him, 'They have no wine.' Jesus said, 'Woman, why turn to me? My hour has not yet come" (John 2:3–4).

Jesus seems to be responding to a different statement. Mary is talking about the acutely embarrassing situation in which the young married couple find themselves since there is no more wine for the wedding feast, but Jesus, by mentioning that "my hour has not yet come", seems to be referring to the hour of his death on the cross.

41

In speaking to his mother, Jesus calls her "woman". The great scripture scholar Raymond Brown commented that in the whole of the Bible and ancient literature there is not a single example, apart from Cana and Calvary, of a son addressing his mother as "woman".[9] He says to her that "his hour has not yet come" – the hour of his death on the cross. And when his hour comes, the hour of our redemption, Jesus uses that same word "woman" to speak to his mother at the foot of the cross when he says, "Woman, this is your son" (John 19:26). Many scholars see in Jesus' use of the word "woman", when addressing his mother, a reference to Eve, "the mother of all the living" (Genesis 3:20), who was also called "woman". Just as Eve is the mother of "all the living", so Mary, by the word of Jesus, becomes the mother of all the redeemed.

The Symbol of Wine

If we stay just on the surface of this story we can miss the deeper symbolism of the "wedding feast" in Cana. For the prophet Isaiah, a shortage of wine represents the people's need and yearning for salvation: "There is lamentation in the streets: no wine, joy quite gone, gladness banished from the country" (Isaiah 24:11).

Does Jesus hear, in his mother's observation that "they have no wine", a reference to the urgent need of salvation for the people? If he does, his response "my hour has not yet come" makes sense. He will have to await the hour of his death and resurrection to bring that salvation. But because the abundance of wine is the prophet's symbol of redemption, Jesus can anticipate his redemptive death by providing, at his mother's request, the symbol of redemption. The prophet said:

> "Yahweh Sabaoth will prepare for all peoples
> a banquet of rich food, a banquet of fine wines
> of food rich and juicy, of fine strained wine.
> On this mountain he will remove

the mourning veil covering all peoples,
and the shroud enwrapping all nations,
he will destroy Death for ever." (Isaiah 25:6–8)

Despite Jesus' apparent refusal to get involved in the embarrassing situation of the lack of wine in Cana, Mary was confident that he would respond to her request. She said to the servants, *"Do whatever he tells you."* Jesus told them to fill with water the six stone water jars that could each hold twenty or thirty gallons. Then he said, "Draw some now and take it to the steward." They did this; the steward tasted the water, and it had turned into wine… "and the steward said to the bridegroom, 'you have kept the best wine till now'" (John 2:5–10). In response to his mother's request, Jesus not only provided enough wine for the wedding party in Cana, he also provided the prophet Isaiah's symbol of salvation in creating an abundance of wine: over a thousand bottles of the "best wine"! St John says, "This was the first of the signs given by Jesus: it was given at Cana in Galilee. He let his glory be seen, and his disciples believed in him" (John 2:11).

Jesus the Bridegroom at the Wedding Feast

We have to re-read the story of the wedding feast in Cana in the light of the prophecy of Amos: "The mountains will run with new wine and the hills all flow with it" (Amos 9:13). The wedding in Cana is about the new wine of salvation that Jesus, the divine bridegroom, brings. John the Baptist had identified Jesus as "the bridegroom" when he said "the bride is only for the bridegroom" (John 3:29). In Scripture, God's people are the bride and God himself is the bridegroom. The prophet Hosea wrote, "In that day, says the Lord, you will call me 'My husband' and no longer call me, 'My Baal'" (Hosea 2:18). And the prophet Isaiah said, "Your Maker is your husband, the Lord of hosts is his name" (Isaiah 54:5). Because of this marriage union between God and his people, sin is always referred to in the Old Testament as the breaking of the vow of marriage, as adultery.

The specific mission of Jesus, the divine bridegroom, is "to save his people from their sins" (Matthew 1:21). Jesus is the bridegroom and the Church is his bride. In providing the abundance of wine, the wine of salvation, for the wedding feast in Cana at the beginning of his public ministry, Jesus shows that God's salvation is at hand. He let his glory as the divine bridegroom bringing salvation to his bride be seen, and that is why his disciples believed in him. As one scripture scholar observes, "When the mother of Jesus says to him, 'They have no wine', she places him in the role of the bridegroom, whose responsibility it is to provide the wine."[10]

When we pray the *Our Father* in this decade, we can linger on the petition "thy kingdom come". We can see in the abundance of wine that Jesus, the bridegroom of God's people, provided for the wedding feast the symbol of God's kingdom. God the "Father of mercies" is fulfilling his promise to redeem his people. As we say our *Hail Marys*, we keep in mind that Jesus anticipated his "hour", at his mother's request, by providing the prophetic sign of wine in abundance and assuming his role as the "bridegroom" of God's people.

Prayer of Intercession

O Mother of Perpetual Succour, obtain for us the grace to make our home in this Mystery of your Son, our Lord Jesus Christ, as we meditate on the great mercy that the "Father of mercies" has shown to us.

The Third Mystery of Light

Jesus Preaches the Gospel

St Mark begins his account of Jesus' preaching with these words: "After John had been arrested, Jesus went into Galilee. There he proclaimed the Good News from God saying, 'The time is fulfilled, and the kingdom of God is close at hand. Repent and believe the Good News'" (Mark 1:14–15). Those words, "Good News", sum up the whole message, the whole revelation of Jesus. He is the bringer of Good News. But what do we mean by news? News is not a history lesson. It is not information about something that happened in the past. Jesus is bringing us the Good News of what God is doing right now. And right now God is offering his love and mercy to each one of us. As Jesus said to Nicodemus, "This is how God loved the world; he gave his only Son, so that everyone who believes may not perish but may have eternal life in him" (John 3:16). This is the Good News we ourselves need to hear today.

Jesus is the Good News

Jesus himself is "the Good News from God". He himself is the kingdom of God. As Pope Francis says:

> Jesus Christ is the face of the Father's mercy. These words might well sum up the mystery of the Christian faith. Mercy has become living and visible in Jesus of Nazareth, reaching its culmination in him.[11]

When we accept the Good News of the Gospel, it is not a theory about life or a philosophy of life that we are accepting. As St Pope John Paul II wrote:

> The Kingdom of God is not a concept, a doctrine, or a

programme subject to free interpretation, but before all else a *person* with the face and name of Jesus of Nazareth, the image of the invisible God.[12]

It is the person of Jesus Christ himself, the incarnate Son of God, who has become our brother, who is the Good News from God. When we accept Jesus we enter the kingdom of God, or, the kingdom of God enters us. Jesus said to us, "The kingdom of God is within you" (Luke 17:21). The Good News of Jesus brings us into a personal relationship with him. As Pope Benedict XVI wrote:

Being a Christian is not the result of an ethical choice or a lofty idea, but an encounter with an event, a person, which gives life a new horizon and a decisive direction.[13]

Jesus, in his very person, embodies the Good News of God the Father's love and mercy, which he also expresses in his encouraging words and merciful deeds. We see his Good News in action as he heals the sick and casts out evil spirits. We also see him manifesting the love and mercy of God as he seeks out the outcasts, the prostitutes and sinners, and sits at their table and shares a meal with them. And we also hear his Good News in his wonderful teaching on such occasions as the Sermon on the Mount. He speaks God's word to us.

God Speaks His Word in the Present

Scripture says "the word of God is something alive and active" (Hebrews 4:12). Jesus speaks that word to us today, and although he physically walked this earth two thousand years ago, his word is alive and active today. When we hear his Gospel proclaimed or when we read the Gospel for ourselves, Jesus speaks directly to us. He makes it clear to us that everything God said to us in the Hebrew Scriptures (Old Testament) is now being fulfilled: "God loved the world so much that he gave his only Son to save the world" (John 3:16). That expresses the reality of God's love. That is the love which embraces and welcomes us when we turn to God. That is the love we experience as we make our home in the Mystery of Christ.

The Gospel which Jesus preaches to us is about the love that God has for us and the mercy he wants to show us. As the psalm says, "As far as the east is from the west, so far does he remove our sins" (Psalm 103:12). When Adam sinned he thought that he had lost his dignity and so, when God went seeking him in the garden, he hid. God asked him why he was hiding and he said, "I was afraid because I was naked" (Genesis 3:10). In the dreadful awareness that he had lost the grace of God, Adam became aware of his nakedness. He feared that he had lost his dignity in God's sight. He had forgotten his true identity.

Christ Fully Reveals Us to Ourselves

Jesus came to reassure us that God in his great love and mercy was restoring to us all our dignity as children of God. The Apostle John said, "You must see what great love the Father has lavished on us by letting us be called God's children which is what we are" (1 John 3:1). Jesus Christ reveals to us that we are God's children and that when we pray we should speak to God as "our Father". The Vatican Council reminded us that "Christ… fully reveals humanity to itself and brings to light its very high calling".[14] Our high calling is to be the sons and daughters of God and to "live through love in God's presence" (Ephesians 1:4). That is surely an amazing dignity. Indeed, St Pope John Paul II could say, "The name for that amazement at man's worth and dignity is the Gospel. It is also called, Christianity…"[15]

The Gospel is about our God-given dignity as God's sons and daughters. We need to welcome this Gospel each new day.

As we "make our home" in this mystery we thank God the Father for sending us Jesus to bring the amazing good news to us that we are truly his beloved children. While we say the *Our Father* we remind ourselves that it was Jesus himself who taught us to say this prayer, to call God our Father. We become aware of the joy in the Father's heart when we confidently come to him as our loving Father.

When Jesus began preaching the Gospel he had to leave home, to leave Mary, his mother, who was probably a widow at that time. Tradition holds that St Joseph died before Jesus began his public ministry. Jesus left his mother's home in Nazareth but Mary found a new home in him. While we say our *Hail Mary*s we remember that Mary, who pondered all the words of Jesus in her heart, was the very first disciple to make her home in him, to live all the mysteries of his life in him. She did what Jesus asks each of us to do: "Make your home in me as I make mine in you" (John 15:4).

Jesus and the Holy Spirit

Jesus performed all his works through the power of the Holy Spirit, through whom he preached, healed the sick, cast out evil spirits and brought us the Gospel.

Our gratitude to the Holy Spirit takes the form of opening our hearts and welcoming the Spirit into the very depths of our being. The prayer that St Paul prays for us expresses this well: "Out of his infinite glory, may the Father give you the power through his Spirit for your hidden self to grow strong, so that Christ may dwell in your hearts through faith, and then, planted in love and built on love, you will with all the saints have strength to grasp the breadth and the length, the height and the depth; until, knowing the love of Christ, which is beyond all knowledge, you are filled with the utter fullness of God" (Ephesians 3:16–19).

Prayer of Intercession

O Mother of Perpetual Succour, obtain for us the grace to make our home in this Mystery of your Son, our Lord Jesus Christ, as we meditate on the great mercy that the "Father of mercies" has shown to us.

The Fourth Mystery of Light
The Transfiguration

Jesus took Peter, James and John up a high mountain to pray. This happened shortly after Peter responded to Jesus' question, "But you, who do you say that I am?" With Peter's confession of faith, "You are the Christ the Son of the living God" (Matthew 16:15–16), Jesus responded to him, "You are a blessed man because it was not flesh and blood that revealed this to you but my Father who is in heaven" (Matthew 16:17). On the mountain the disciples received a visible manifestation of the truth that Peter professed. While Jesus was at prayer on the mountain, the Gospel tells us, "the aspect of his face altered, and his clothing became brilliant as lightning. Suddenly there were two men there talking with him; they were Moses and Elijah appearing in glory, and they were speaking of his passing which he was to accomplish in Jerusalem" (Luke 9:29–31).

The New Exodus

"His passing" literally means "his Exodus", a word that connects Jesus' approaching passion and death with that first Exodus of God's people when Moses, who is now talking to Jesus on the mountain, led them from slavery in Egypt into freedom. The death of Jesus will be the "second Exodus" of God's people, not into an earthly kingdom, but into the kingdom of God. The salvation symbolised by the first Exodus is about to be realised in Jesus' Exodus from this world to the glory of the Father.

Moses and the great prophet Elijah are talking to Jesus about his approaching passion and death. Pope Benedict XVI wrote:

> Their topic of conversation is the cross, but understood in the inclusive sense of Jesus' Exodus, which had to take place in Jerusalem. Jesus' cross is an Exodus: a departure from this life, a passage through the "Red Sea" of the Passion and a transition into glory – glory, however, that forever bears the mark of Jesus' wounds.[16]

"Beholding this glory, Peter spoke up and said, 'Master, it is wonderful for us to be here; so let us make three tents, one for you, one for Moses and one for Elijah.' As he spoke a cloud came and covered them with shadow; and when the disciples entered the cloud they were afraid. And a voice came from the cloud and said, 'This is my Son, the Chosen One. Listen to him'" (Luke 9:33–35).

Listen to Him

At his baptism, God the Father said to Jesus, "You are my beloved Son in whom I am well pleased" (Luke 3:22). On the Mountain of the Transfiguration, the Father says to the disciples, "Listen to him" (Luke 9:35). In the first Exodus from slavery, God's people listened to Moses and Elijah. Now, in the new Exodus of our liberation from sin, accomplished by Jesus on the cross, God the Father tells us to listen to him. Pope Benedict XVI commented: "We constantly have to let the Lord draw us into his conversation with Moses and Elijah; we constantly have to learn from him, the Risen Lord, to understand the Scripture afresh."[17]

Each day we have to listen afresh to him.

Witnessing the transfiguration of Jesus on the mountain was a most profound experience for the three disciples. It is first and foremost an experience of what happens when Jesus prays. Because this mystery of the transfiguration is an experience of Jesus at prayer, it can also become for us a great "prayer event" as we behold, in our meditation, the glory of God shining on the face of Jesus. Jesus said of himself, "I am the light of the world. If you follow me you will not walk in darkness" (John 8:12).

For his three chosen disciples, Jesus lets that light shine in a most remarkable way. Peter could never forget it. In his second letter to the Churches he wrote, "He was honoured and glorified by God the Father, when a voice came to him from the transcendent Glory: *This is my Son, the Beloved; he enjoys my favour*. We ourselves heard this voice from heaven, when we were with him on the holy mountain" (2 Peter 1:17–18).

We Shall Be Like Him

In our meditation we are not analysing what is happening. Rather, we are allowing Christ's transfiguration to speak to us and to enlighten our minds and hearts as we contemplate this mystery. St John, who was with Peter and James on the mountain, tells us, "We are already the children of God, but what we are to be in the future has not yet been revealed to us; all we know is that when it is revealed we shall be like him because we shall see him as he really is" (1 John 3:2). In the face of the transfigured Christ we catch a glimpse of how our own humanity will be transformed when Christ comes again in glory.

The glory of the Father, shining on the face of Jesus, is the central focus of our contemplation while we say the *Our Father* at the beginning of this decade. The presence of Moses and Elijah talking with Jesus about "his Exodus" reminds us vividly that the cross and resurrection are the way of this Exodus.

While saying our *Hail Marys*, we gaze on this same glory with the eyes of Mary, his mother. She teaches us to ponder these mysteries in our hearts. She will remind us that Jesus' "Exodus" did not take place on the Mountain of the Transfiguration but on the hill of Calvary. The words that Jesus spoke to Nicodemus were pondered deeply by his mother: "The Son of Man must be lifted up as Moses lifted up the serpent in the desert, so that everyone who believes may have eternal life in him" (John 3:13–14).

Prayer of Intercession

O Mother of Perpetual Succour, obtain for us the grace to make our home in this Mystery of your Son, our Lord Jesus Christ, as we meditate on the great mercy that the "Father of mercies" has shown to us.

The Fifth Mystery of Light

Jesus Gives Us the Eucharist

The mystery of the Eucharist is at the very heart of our faith. Jesus said about himself, "I am the living bread which has come down from heaven. Anyone who eats this bread will live for ever; and the bread that I shall give is my flesh for the life of the world" (John 6:51). Many of his disciples who had been following him until then objected strongly to what Jesus was saying, but he continued, with still greater emphasis, "I tell you most solemnly, if you do not eat the flesh of the Son of Man and drink his blood you will not have life in you. Anyone who eats my flesh and drinks my blood has eternal life and I shall raise him up on the last day. For my flesh is real food and my blood is real drink. He who eats my flesh and drinks my blood lives in me and I live in him" (John 6:53–56).

Hearing Jesus spell out so clearly that he was serious about giving us his flesh and blood as the food of eternal life, many of his disciples left him, saying, "This is intolerable language and who can believe it?" (John 6:60). Jesus didn't try to stop them leaving. Rather, he even said to the Twelve, "What about you, do you want to go away too?" (John 6:67). He was prepared to let the Twelve depart if they did not accept that he would give us his flesh to eat and his blood to drink.

Those disillusioned disciples who walked away were not present at the Last Supper when Jesus gave us himself as "the bread of life". As the Gospel records, "When evening came he was at table with the Twelve… Now as they were eating, Jesus took bread, and when he had said the blessing he broke it and gave it to the disciples. 'Take it and eat it,' he said, 'this is my body.' Then he took a cup and when he had returned thanks he gave it to them. 'Drink all of you from this,' he said, 'for this is my blood, the blood of the covenant, which is to be poured out for many for the forgiveness of sins'" (Matthew 26:20, 26–28).

The Mystery of Faith

This is the great mystery of our faith. It is the mystery which sums up in itself everything that God has done through Christ for our salvation. Christ our Saviour is truly present on the altar, under the appearance of bread and wine, so that he can fulfil his promise, "He who eats my flesh and drinks my blood lives in me and I live in him" (John 6:56). St John Paul II wrote:

> When the Church celebrates the Eucharist, the memorial of her Lord's death and resurrection, this central event of salvation becomes really present and "the work of our redemption is carried out". This sacrifice is so decisive for the salvation of the human race that Jesus Christ offered

it and returned to the Father only *after he had left us a means of sharing in it* as if we had been present there."[18]

Notice those words "as if we had been present there". Christ's love for each of us is such that he has made it possible for us to be present at the very act of our redemption. That is what the Mass is: the very presence of Christ, under the appearance of bread and wine, as he offers himself, an eternal offering never to be repeated, to his Father for our salvation. Christ's great sacrifice is not something that belongs to past history. Because it is eternally in God's presence, it becomes present to us under the appearance of bread and wine in the Mass. Reflecting on this great mystery of our faith, St Alphonsus de' Liguori exclaimed:

> If anything could shake my faith in the Eucharist it would not be the doubt as to how bread and wine could become flesh... because I should answer that God can do everything; but if I ask myself how could he love us so much as to make himself our food, I can only answer that this is a mystery of faith above my comprehension, and that the love of Jesus cannot be understood.[19]

Through the Power of the Holy Spirit

Christ becomes truly present, under the appearance of bread and wine on the altar, through the same power by which he truly became man in his mother's womb – through the power of the Holy Spirit. When Mary asked the archangel Gabriel how she, as a virgin, could become a mother, she was told, "The Holy Spirit will come upon you and the power of the Most High will cover you with its shadow" (Luke 1:35). We invoke that same power over our gifts of bread and wine on the altar when the priest raises his hands and prays, "Make holy, therefore, these gifts, we pray, by sending down your Spirit upon them like the dewfall, so that they may become for us the body and blood of our Lord, Jesus Christ."[20] As Pope Francis says, "The Lord, in the culmination of the mystery of the Incarnation, chose to reach our intimate depths through a fragment of matter."[21]

We Become the Eucharist We Celebrate

In offering our gift of bread and wine to God at Mass we are offering ourselves, our whole being, everything about us. When the Holy Spirit comes upon our gift, "the mystery of faith" becomes present, and the bread and wine that represent us before God become, for us, the very Body and Blood of Christ.

The Eucharist is the sacrament Jesus gave to us at his Last Supper so that he can now enter into our hearts in Holy Communion and so transform us that we become his body in this world. He comes to each of us in his risen and glorified body, uniting us so intimately with himself that we become his body. St Leo the Great said, "Our partaking of the Body and Blood of Christ tends only to make us become what we eat."[22] We eat the Body of Christ and we become the Body of Christ in this world. We become the Eucharist we celebrate.

As we pray the *Our Father* we can linger for a moment on our request, "Give us this day our daily bread." The bread of the Eucharist is our "daily bread" for our spiritual growth and strength. We thank the Father for this gift of Jesus. We also remember that it is through the outpouring of the Holy Spirit on our gifts of bread and wine that they become for us the Body and Blood of Christ and we give praise to the Spirit of God. And as we say the *Hail Mary*s, we join the mother of Jesus in pondering this great mystery in our hearts.

Prayer of Intercession

O Mother of Perpetual Succour, obtain for us the grace to make our home in this Mystery of your Son, our Lord Jesus Christ, as we meditate on the great mercy that the "Father of mercies" has shown to us.

Chapter Four

The Sorrowful Mysteries

The First Sorrowful Mystery

The Agony in the Garden

St Matthew concludes his account of the Last Supper and the gift of the Holy Eucharist with these words: "After the psalms had been sung they left for the Mount of Olives" (Matthew 26:30). Jesus was singing hymns of praise and thanks to God on his way to the garden of Gethsemane. In giving us the gift of the Holy Eucharist he had offered himself sacrificially to the Father with the words, "Drink from this all of you, for this is my blood, the blood of the covenant, poured out for many for the forgiveness of sins" (Matthew 26:27–28). Now he knows that out of his love for the Father and for us he will have to endure the long hours of his passion. The religious authorities have rejected him, refused to accept the good news he brought to the people from God his Father; refused to accept that he came from God, and so they were determined to put him to death. The death sentence that they demanded Pilate to pass was not God's will. God's will was that Jesus would bring to all people the Good News of our salvation. By faithfully doing that, Jesus incurred the enmity and the rejection of sinful humanity and, finally, the death sentence that it passed on him.

His Agony

Jesus took with him the three disciples, Peter, James and John, who were present when he was transfigured on the mountain, as he withdrew from the other disciples to pray. He said to them, "My soul is sorrowful to the point of death. Wait here and stay awake with me" (Matthew 26:38). He needed their support at that moment. He knew that he was, in the words of John the Baptist, "the lamb of God who takes away the sin of the world" (John 1:29). He knew, as he said to the disciples that "the words of scripture are destined to be fulfilled in me" (Luke 22:37), the words spoken by the prophet Isaiah: "He was despised, the lowest of men, a man of sorrows, familiar with suffering, one from whom, as it were, we averted our gaze, despised, for whom we had no regard" (Isaiah 53:3). Jesus knew that he had to face a time of horrendous suffering, pain and death. That dreadful awareness filled his whole being with anguish and terror. He fell on his face and cried out to his Father, "If you are willing, take this cup away from me. Nevertheless, let your will be done, not mine" (Luke 22:42).

His agony was real. St Luke says, "In his anguish he prayed even more earnestly, and his sweat fell to the ground like drops of blood" (Luke 22:44). Jesus was not a "superman" who could not be touched by human suffering. Jesus, in being born into this world, as St Paul says, "emptied himself, taking the form of a slave, becoming as human beings are" (Philippians 2:7).

Your Will Be Done

In his humanity, Jesus feels all the anguish and terror of his approaching passion. In his baptism at the Jordan by John the Baptist, Jesus identified himself totally with our sinful humanity. As Pope Benedict XVI explained, "Jesus loaded the burdens of mankind's guilt upon his shoulders; he bore it down into the depths of the Jordan. He inaugurated his public activity by stepping into the place of sinners. His inaugural gesture is an anticipation of the cross."[23]

Now, in the Garden of Gethsemane, after giving us the gift of himself in the Holy Eucharist, Jesus experiences the bitter horror of the human condition, cut off from God by sin and evil. Redemption from this dreadful situation is necessary. As he said to Nicodemus, "Yes, God loved the world so much that he gave his only Son, so that everyone who believes in him may not be lost but may have eternal life. For God sent his Son into the world not to condemn the world, but so that through him the world might be saved" (John 3:16–17). Now the hour of our salvation has arrived, and as he experiences the bitter agony of our sinfulness he sweats blood and prays, "Abba, Father, for you everything is possible. Take this cup from me. But let it be as you, not I, would have it" (Mark 14:36).

In his transfiguration on the mountain, Moses and Elijah talked to him about "the Exodus" that he would accomplish in Jerusalem (Luke 9:30–31), the "new Exodus", when he would lead God's people into the kingdom of God. Now his hour has come and he submits his human will to God's will. He says the prayer that his mother said when she consented to become his mother: "Let it happen to me as you have said" (Luke 1:38). Many times during his preaching Jesus said, "I have come from heaven, not to do my own will, but to do the will of the one who sent me" (John 6:38).

The will of the Father is for Jesus to lead us in the "new Exodus" into the kingdom of God. But Jesus' enemies, and especially the evil one, Satan, are determined to destroy him, by having him condemned to the horrible death by crucifixion. Facing this time of horrendous suffering, Jesus prayed to the Father "Your will be done" and an angel came "and gave him strength" (Luke 22:42, 43). St John concludes his account of the agony in Gethsemane with these words: "Knowing everything that was to happen to him Jesus came forward and said (*to those who had come to arrest him*), 'Who are you looking for?' They answered, 'Jesus the Nazarene.' He said, 'I am he.' When Jesus said, 'I am he,' they moved back and fell to the ground" (John 18:4–6). After his agony Jesus faces his captors with serenity and dignity. They are the ones who fall to the ground as he proclaims, "I am he." But he allows them to take him prisoner.

As we "make our home'" in this mystery, we can open our hearts in love and sympathy with Jesus as he struggles with the Father's will. Could there not be another way to save the human race? Jesus gives us permission to struggle with God's will in our lives as he did in his. As he faced the horrendous suffering that lay ahead of him he prayed that it might pass. When we are faced with suffering in our own lives, we too can pray that it might pass. But, like Jesus, we too hope that we will say his prayer, "Abba, Father, for you everything is possible. Take this cup from me. But let it be as you, not I, would have it" (Mark 14:36). And as we say that prayer, an angel of God will give us strength just as he gave Jesus strength.

While saying the *Our Father* at the beginning of this first decade of the Sorrowful Mysteries, we remind ourselves that Jesus taught us this prayer and taught us to say to the Father the prayer he said during his agony in Gethsemane, "Thy will be done." Jesus' prayer brought salvation to the human race. Our prayer that the Father's will might be done will bring us great blessings.

The Mother of Sorrows

As we say the *Hail Marys*, our hearts go out to the mother of Jesus. Her beloved Son was now prostrate in Gethsemane, overcome with anguish as he faced the hour of our salvation. Mary knew what Isaiah had foretold: "Ours were the sufferings he was bearing, ours the sorrow he was carrying" (Isaiah 53:4). Mary had pondered well those words that Simeon spoke to her when she presented the child Jesus in the Temple: "he is destined for the fall and the rise of many in Israel, destined to be a sign that is opposed – and a sword will pierce your soul too – so that the secret thoughts of many may be laid bare" (Luke 2:34–35). As the passion and death of Jesus unfold, Mary becomes "the Mother of Sorrows".

Mary would have taught the young boy Jesus to say to God his Father, "Your will be done." Now, in her own agony, as her heart is one with the heart of Jesus, she prays to God the Father, "Your will be done." In her darkest moment of desolation Mary believed "that the promises made to her by the Lord would be fulfilled" (Luke 1:45).

Prayer of Intercession

O Mother of Perpetual Succour, obtain for us the grace to make our home in this Mystery of your Son, our Lord Jesus Christ, as we meditate on the great mercy that the "Father of mercies" has shown to us.

The Second Sorrowful Mystery
The Scourging at the Pillar

From his agony in the garden, Jesus, arrested on the orders of "the chief priests and elders", was "led to the house of Caiaphas the High Priest, where the scribes and elders were assembled" (Matthew 26:47, 57). Jesus threatened their whole way of life because his view of the Kingdom of God totally opposed theirs.

Jesus was put on trial before the Sanhedrin, the supreme council or court in ancient Israel. St Matthew says, "The chief priests and the whole Sanhedrin were looking for evidence against Jesus, however false, on which they might have him executed. But they could not find any, though several lying witnesses came forward" (Matthew 26:59–60). Caiaphas the high priest then said to Jesus, "I put you on oath by the living God to tell us if you are the Christ, the Son of God" (Matthew 26:63). When Jesus said "Yes", they had the evidence they needed. Jesus responded to Caiaphas with the words, "It is you who say it. But I tell you that from this time onward you will see the *Son of Man seated at the right hand of the power and coming on the clouds of heaven"* (Matthew 26:64). Caiaphas now had the evidence he needed and he said triumphantly to those assembled in the court, "You have just heard the blasphemy. What is your opinion?" They answered, "He deserves to die" (Matthew 26:65–66). Notice that it was the religious leaders who condemned Jesus to death because he bore witness to the truth that he was indeed "the Christ, the Son of God".

Jesus was then brought before Pilate, the Roman governor, who alone had the civil authority to sentence a man to death. During his interrogation of Jesus, Pilate, who would have known from his own security services that Jesus posed no military threat to the Roman Empire, asked him, "Are you the king of the Jews?" Jesus replied, "Mine is not a kingdom of this world." Pilate responded, "So, then, you are a king?" Jesus answered, "It is you who say that I am a king. I was born for this. I came into the world for this, to bear witness to the truth; and all who are on the side of truth listen to my voice." "Truth," said Pilate, "what is that?" (John 18:33–38). Jesus, who said of himself, "I am the Truth" (John 14:6), is now being asked "what is truth?"!

Pilate then went out and said to the crowd clamouring for the death of Jesus, "I find no case against this man" (John 19:38). But instead of releasing Jesus, he gave the crowd the "amnesty option", thereby placing Jesus, against whom he could find no grounds for condemnation, in the same category as a man who had been condemned to death. He said to the crowd: "According to a custom of yours I should release one prisoner at Passover: would you like me to release for you the king of the Jews?" At this they shouted, "Not this man, but Barabbas" (John 18:39–40). Sadly, these words of the crowd have been attributed to the whole Jewish people, but as Pope Benedict XVI rightly pointed out:

> The Barabbas party, the crowd, was conspicuous, while the followers of Jesus remained hidden out of fear; this meant that the *vox populi,* on which Roman law was built, was represented one-sidedly. In Mark's account, then, in addition to "the Jews", that is the dominant priestly circle, the *ochlos* (the crowd) comes into play, the circle of Barabbas' supporters, but not the Jewish people as such.[24]

Pilate then released Barabbas and "had Jesus taken away and scourged" (John 19:1).

Scourging: the most barbaric torture

Writing about this cruel practice of scourging, Pope Benedict XVI said:

> In ancient Roman criminal law scourging was the

punishment that accompanied the death sentence. In John's Gospel, however, it is presented as an act during the interrogation, a measure the Prefect was empowered to take on the basis of his responsibility for law enforcement. It was an extremely barbaric punishment: the victim was struck by several torturers, for as long as it took them to grow tired, and for the flesh of the criminal to hang down in bleeding shreds.[25]

As we contemplate Jesus in this sorrowful mystery of his scourging, we are speechless at the horrors of his suffering. He truly has become "the man of sorrows" (Isaiah 53:3). We cannot, however, remain detached from his suffering, as if it had nothing to do with us. As the prophet had foretold, "Ours were the sufferings he was bearing, ours the sorrows he was carrying" (Isaiah 53:4).

We "make our home" in this mystery of Christ, remembering that it was for us and for our salvation that Jesus is now undergoing such terrible suffering. We contemplate the love that Christ has for us and we repent of our own lack of love for him. He is dying so that we may live with God the Father for ever. Christ's scourging reveals the horrible corruption of sin, of being cut off from God. Sin always seeks to destroy goodness, to kill Christ. We have been wounded by that sin and we need the redemption that Christ's passion and death won for us. St Peter says to us, "Through his bruises you have been healed" (1 Peter 2:24–25). All of Christ's sufferings were for us and for our salvation.

The Father's Love

While saying the *Our Father* of this decade we remember that it is the Father's love for us, as well as Jesus' love, that is manifested in his suffering. Jesus said, "For this is how God loved the world: he gave his only Son, so that everyone who believes in him may not perish but may have eternal life" (John 3:16). Our salvation is the gift of the Father, won for us through the great love manifested by Jesus in his terrible suffering at the hands of sinful humanity.

As we "make our home" in this mystery we open our hearts in gratitude to the Father and we ask forgiveness for all our own sins against his love and against Jesus.

Through Mary's Eyes

While praying the *Hail Marys* we can contrast in our mind, just for a moment, the beautiful phrase "Blessed is the fruit of your womb, Jesus" with the picture of his body now being shredded under the lashes of the scourging. The "fruit of her womb" has become "the Man of Sorrows" and she has become "the Mother of Sorrows". We can only gaze in sorrow at such suffering.

Mary, the Mother of Sorrows, remained steadfast in her faith. Mary is seeing the terrible passion of Jesus through the eyes of his loving Father. To use a human expression of God the Father, we can say that his heart was broken by what the sins of humanity had done to his incarnate Son. And Mary's heart was also broken by that terrible crime. But Mary remained at one with the will of the Father, because she believed in the Father's love and mercy for all human beings. Although her heart was now broken in agony for her Son, "she believed that the promise made to her by the Lord would be fulfilled" (Luke 1·45).

Despite this dark mystery of Christ's suffering, we believe with Mary that the Holy Spirit, the Lord and giver of life, and not Caiaphas or Pilate, will have the last word on the life and mission of Jesus.

We conclude our meditation on this sorrowful mystery with the confident praise of the Trinity as we say, *Glory be to the Father and to the Son and to the Holy Spirit.*

Prayer of Intercession

O Mother of Perpetual Succour, obtain for us the grace to make our home in this Mystery of your Son, our Lord Jesus Christ, as we meditate on the great mercy that the "Father of mercies" has shown to us.

The Third Sorrowful mystery
The Crowning with Thorns

The pain and suffering inflicted on Jesus by the torture of the scourging didn't satisfy his sadistic tormentors. St Matthew writes, "The soldiers took Jesus with them into the Praetorium and collected the whole cohort round him. And they stripped him and put a scarlet cloak round him, and having twisted some thorns into a crown, they put this on his head and placed a reed in his right hand. To make fun of him they knelt to him saying, 'Hail, king of the Jews.' And they spat on him and took the reed and struck him on the head with it" (Matthew 27:27–30). They mocked the King of Kings.

In the horror of this painful abuse we can see a deeper reality as we focus on the crown, albeit of thorns, which is placed on Jesus' head. Jesus said to the two disciples on the road to Emmaus, on that first Easter morning, "'You foolish men! So slow to believe the full message of the prophets. Was it not ordained that the Christ should suffer and so enter into his glory?' Then, starting with Moses and going through the prophets, he explained to them the passages throughout the scriptures that were about himself" (Luke 24:25–27).

Everything that the scriptures foretold about Christ had to be fulfilled.

The scriptures said that the Messiah would be the "bridegroom" of God's people. Although those soldiers were mocking Christ's claim to be a king, as they placed the crown of thorns on his head, they were also identifying Jesus as the bridegroom.

Crowns were worn not only by kings but also by Jewish bridegrooms on the day of their wedding. Jesus was not only king – he was also the "divine bridegroom" of God's sinful people. John the Baptist said to his own disciples, "The bride is only for the bridegroom; and yet the bridegroom's friend, who stands there and listens, is glad when he hears the bridegroom's voice" (John 3:29). The Baptist identified Jesus as "the bridegroom". Jesus too identified himself as the bridegroom. When the Pharisees complained to Jesus that his disciples didn't fast, Jesus responded, "Surely the bridegroom's attendants cannot fast while the bridegroom is still with them? As long as they have the bridegroom with them, they cannot fast. But the time will come when the bridegroom is taken away from them, and then, on that day, they will fast" (Mark 2:19–20).

The Bridegroom is Recognised by His Crown

Jesus, in the midst of his scourging, is about to be taken away to "consummate" his marriage on the cross and so he wears his crown. The bridegroom is recognised by his crown. As one biblical scholar writes, "The way any first-century Jew would recognise the bridegroom was to look for the man wearing the crown. As Jewish scholar Michael Satlow puts it, "the ancient Jewish bridegroom was a king for a day".[26] We see, beneath the horrible suffering of the "crown of thorns" and the mockery, the divine bridegroom's love for his bride, for God's sinful people. As the psalm says, "He crowns you with faithful love and tenderness" (Psalm 103:4). Jesus wears the crown of thorns so that we can wear the crown of his "faithful love and tenderness".

The Spousal Love of Christ

Scripture employs the image of the tender, self-giving love of the bridegroom for his bride to help us to contemplate the love of Christ, especially as he endures his passion for us. As we contemplate Christ in his passion, crowned with thorns, we see in the midst of such terrible barbarity the love of "the divine bridegroom" for his sinful bride, our fallen human race.

An Amazing Love Story

While we say the *Our Father* we remind ourselves that the whole history of our salvation is a divine love story between God and his people.

It is the Father's love that Jesus reveals as he wears his crown of thorns. The hour of "the wedding feast of the Lamb" has come. The "wedding feast of the Lamb" will be celebrated and consummated on the cross as Jesus offers his life for the salvation of his bride. That instrument of torture and mockery, the crown of thorns, becomes for us the symbol of the divine bridegroom's total giving of himself to his bride, the Church.

While saying the *Hail Mary*s we keep in mind this great spousal love which Jesus had for us and we may linger on our petition to our Blessed Mother as we say "pray for us sinners". Mary always pondered what the angel said to Joseph about the child: "He will save his people from their sins" (Matthew 1:21). She always prays for us sinners. And nothing gives her greater joy than for us to invoke her intercession for sinners. She always remains ready to respond because she is the Mother of Perpetual Succour.

We keep in mind this divine, spousal love of God, manifested in

Jesus the bridegroom, as we conclude this decade with our Trinitarian prayer of praise: *Glory be to the Father, the Son and the Holy Spirit.*

Prayer of Intercession

O Mother of Perpetual Succour, obtain for us the grace to make our home in this Mystery of your Son, our Lord Jesus Christ, as we meditate on the great mercy that the "Father of mercies" has shown to us.

The Fourth Sorrowful Mystery
The Carrying of the Cross

Making "the Stations of the Cross" is a very ancient Catholic devotion. We begin with Jesus receiving his cross, after Pilate condemns him to death, and we walk with him along the road to Calvary. On the road he falls three times; he meets his Blessed Mother; Simon is forced to carry the cross because Jesus, weakened by the scourging, has no strength left; the women of Jerusalem weep for him and he comforts them; Veronica wipes the blood off his face with a towel; when he reaches Calvary he is stripped of his garments as the soldiers prepare to nail him to the cross.

In "making our home" in this fourth sorrowful mystery of the Rosary we accompany Jesus to Calvary and we gaze on his suffering, through the eyes of his mother Mary, who was on the journey with him.

The Stations of the Cross

St Alphonsus de' Liguori's meditations on the Stations of the Cross became universally loved in the Catholic Church. He begins with this prayer:

> My Lord Jesus Christ, you willingly walked this painful journey to your death on the Cross with unconditional love for each one of us, and I, how often have I ungratefully abandoned you. But now I love you with my whole soul, and because I love you I am sincerely sorry for having offended you. My Jesus, pardon me and permit me to accompany you on this journey. You are going to die for love of me and it is my wish also, my dearest Redeemer, to die for love of you. My Jesus, in your love I wish to live. In your love I wish to die.[27]

St Alphonsus' prayer, "You are going to die for love of me", creates the contemplative ethos for our accompaniment of Jesus on the road to Calvary and his death on the cross.

Accepting Responsibility

Jesus died because of human sinfulness. St Alphonsus teaches us to take responsibility when he prays, "My loving Jesus, it was not Pilate; no, it was my sins that condemned you to die."[28] It is with a repentant heart that we accompany Jesus and walk with Mary along this sorrowful road. When the sin of Adam and Eve (and our own sins) separated us from the all-holy God, the merciful Father sent his own Son, as "the divine Bridegroom", born of Mary, to become a human being like us in all things. He took upon himself all the sinfulness of "his bride", God's people.

Through his infinite, spousal love, Jesus unites us to himself in a new and eternal covenant and restores us to friendship with God. As Pope Benedict XVI wrote: "Because infinite good is now at hand in the man Jesus, the counterweight to all wickedness is present and active within world history. Good is always infinitely greater than the vast mass of evil, however terrible it may be."[29]

That infinite goodness and mercy that Jesus brings us from God the Father renews and makes us new. But to be touched and transformed by the Father's love and mercy we have to accept Jesus in faith and open our hearts to receive his Spirit.

The New Exodus

In accompanying Jesus along the road to Calvary, as he wears his "bridegroom's crown", the crown of thorns, we walk a road that leads not just to his death in this world, but also to the new life that God promised us: our redemption, our freedom, our liberation, our eternal life in God's kingdom. Jesus leads us in a new "Exodus" from our slavery to sin. When Moses and Elijah came to Jesus during his transfiguration on the mountain, they talked about "the Exodus" that he would accomplish in Jerusalem (Luke 9:31).

Every painful step that Jesus takes along the road to Calvary is a step towards our new life in the Spirit. As we accompany him and his mother we are walking towards the glory of God.

While saying the *Our Father* we keep in mind that it is the Father who is glorifying Christ by giving him to us as our redeemer, and we pray in thanksgiving. This gift of Jesus as our redeemer is the supreme gift of "the Father of mercies".

We pray too with Mary, the mother of Jesus, as we "make our home" in this mystery, and walk with her along this painful journey to Calvary. Our hearts are full of compassion for our sorrowful mother, but we remind ourselves too that Mary's spirit and will are one with her Son and her heart still sings, "His mercy reaches from age to age for those who fear him" (Luke 1:50). Mary believes the word of the prophets and she believes in the redemptive suffering that her Son is undergoing. She has "made her home" in the Mystery of her Son. She is still living her consent to God's will: "let it happen to me as you have said" (Luke 1:38). With Mary, we conclude this meditation as we pray, *Glory be to the Father and to the Son and to the Holy Spirit.*

Prayer of Intercession

O Mother of Perpetual Succour, obtain for us the grace to make our home in this Mystery of your Son, our Lord Jesus Christ, as we meditate on the great mercy that the "Father of mercies" has shown to us.

The Fifth Sorrowful Mystery
The Crucifixion and Death of Jesus

As we "make our home"' in this mystery of Christ's crucifixion and death on the cross, we are flooded with many emotions and many connections with everything we believe about the love of God and our salvation. Jesus' own words about his sacrificial death at the Last Supper live for ever in our hearts: "This is my blood, the blood of the covenant, which is to be poured out for many for the forgiveness of sins" (Matthew 26:28).

The Greatest Act of Love

St Paul in one line sets the tone for our final meditation on the Sorrowful Mysteries. He said, "Jesus Christ was handed over to death for our sins and raised to life for our justification" (Romans 4:25). When we stand beneath the cross of Jesus, we do so in the awareness that the suffering and death of Jesus was also the greatest act of love that he could make for our salvation.

The human race was in bondage to sin, the sin of our first parents and our own sins. This evil of sin distorts God's creation, disfigures the image and likeness of God in human beings. God's response to this distortion of his image and likeness in us was to become one of us in Christ, so that in and through Christ, the "divine bridegroom", the marriage of God and his people could be consummated in an eternal covenant.

The Church Born from the Side of Christ

Christ is the "divine bridegroom" and the Church is his bride. On the cross, as he poured out the last drop of his blood, Christ formed with the Church, his bride, an unbreakable and an everlasting "marriage bond". As the Second Vatican Council teaches, "It was from the side of Christ as he slept the sleep of death on the Cross that there came forth the wondrous sacrament of the whole Church."[30]

The cruel sentence to death by crucifixion that Pilate passed on Jesus had a very different meaning in God's plan for our salvation. Jesus saw his approaching death in this way: "When I am lifted up from the earth I will draw all people to myself" (John 12:32). As we contemplate Christ being lifted up on the cross we willingly and gratefully allow him to draw us into his redeeming love.

Father Forgive Them

As Jesus hung in agony on the cross, his first thought was for those who had condemned him and crucified him. He prayed, "Father, forgive them; they do not know what they are doing" (Luke 23:34). Now he is modelling for us what he taught us to pray in the Our Father: "Forgive us our trespasses as we forgive those who trespass against us." Not only does Jesus forgive them, he also makes excuses for them: "they do not know what they are doing" (Luke 23:34).

After Jesus' resurrection and ascension into heaven, St Peter will make that same excuse when he says to the people in Jerusalem, "Now I know, brothers, that neither you nor your leaders had any idea what you were really doing; this was the way God carried out what he had foretold, when he said through all his prophets that the Christ must suffer" (Acts 3:17–18). St Paul was able to make the same excuse for his own bitter persecution of Christians before his conversion on the road to Damascus. He wrote, "I used to be a blasphemer and did all I could to injure and discredit the faith. Mercy, however, was shown to me, because until I became a believer I had been acting in ignorance; and the grace of our Lord filled me with faith and the love that is in Christ Jesus" (1 Timothy 1:13–14).

She is Your Mother

From the cross, Jesus speaks his last word to his mother and to "the disciple whom he loved", just before he dies. He said to his mother, "Woman, he is your son." He then said to the disciple, "She is your mother." St John tells us, "From that hour the disciple took her into his home" (John 19:27). Pope Benedict XVI comments: "The literal translation is stronger still; it could be rendered like this: he took her into his own – received her into his inner life-setting." Mary became the mother of all disciples, the mother of the Church.

St Alphonsus, writing about Jesus' last word to "the beloved disciple", said:

> Here observe well that Jesus Christ did not address himself to John, but to the disciple, in order to show that he gave Mary to all who are his disciples, that is to say to all Christians, that she might be their Mother. John is but the name of one, whereas the word disciple is applicable to all; therefore our Lord makes use of a name common to all, to show that Mary was given as Mother to all.[32]

At the Last Supper, Jesus gave us the gift of his Body and Blood in the Holy Eucharist. From the cross, at the moment of his death, he gave us the gift of his mother to be our mother. In speaking to her from the cross he called her "Woman", just as he did at the marriage feast at Cana. As Pope Benedict XVI points out:

> The two scenes are linked together. Cana had been an anticipation of the definitive marriage feast – of the new wine that the Lord wanted to bestow. What had then been merely a prophetic sign now becomes a reality.[33]

The Church prays in the Preface of the Mass for the Exaltation of the Holy Cross in this way: "You placed the salvation of the human race on the wood of the cross, so that where death arose, life might again spring forth and the evil one, who conquered on a tree, might likewise on a tree be conquered. Adam and Eve lost the gift of eternal life when, at the devil's tempting, they ate the forbidden fruit of the 'tree of knowledge of good and evil' in the Garden of Eden [Genesis 3:1–19]. Now, from the tree on which Christ died, that life has been restored."

While praying the *Our Father* we consciously "make our home" in this mystery of the crucifixion and death of Jesus, reminding ourselves, in the words of Pope Francis, that "Jesus Christ is the face of the Father's mercy. These words might well sum up the mystery of the Christian faith. Mercy has become living and visible in Jesus of Nazareth, reaching its culmination in him."[34]

Christ's death on the cross is the mystery of God the Father's redeeming love through which he embraces us with his mercy and through which he reconciles us to himself. As we pray "Hallowed be thy name", we can pause for a moment and see how God has truly hallowed his name by redeeming us through the blood of Christ.

We stand with Mary at the foot of the cross and say our *Hail Marys*. The sword that Simeon had foretold has indeed pierced her soul.

But something else has penetrated her soul too – the very last word that Jesus spoke to her, a word she can never forget and a word that has totally transformed her relationship with us. Jesus declared that his mother, through his redeeming death, had become our mother. It is, therefore, with our own spiritual mother Mary that we take our stand at the foot of the cross.

Prayer of Intercession

O Mother of Perpetual Succour, obtain for us the grace to make our home in this Mystery of your Son, our Lord Jesus Christ, as we meditate on the great mercy that the "Father of mercies" has shown to us.

Chapter Five

The Glorious Mysteries

The First Glorious Mystery

The Resurrection of Our Lord

St Paul tells us that "Jesus was put to death for our sins and raised to life to justify us" (Romans 4:25). As we "make our home" in the mystery of Christ's triumph over death we keep in mind that his resurrection was for our justification, for our resurrection into the new life that he brings us.

Christ's resurrection from the dead is the mystery that proclaims not just his own individual triumph over death, but our resurrection too.

The resurrection of Jesus throws a whole new light on his passion and death on the cross. Jesus came to save us from eternal death, the result of sin, through his own death on the cross. God the Father's response to this great love of Jesus for him and for us was to pour out on the dead Jesus the Holy Spirit and raise him into the new life, the new world of the resurrection.

The resurrection of Jesus is the guarantee of our own future resurrection. It is the central mystery of our faith. It is the new creation of our very humanity in Christ. As St Paul said, "Anyone who is in Christ is a new creation; the old creation has gone, and a new one is here. It is all God's work" (2 Corinthians 5:17–18).

The Father's Response to the Crucifixion

In praying this decade of the Rosary, we "make our home" in the mystery of Christ breaking the bonds of death, establishing the new creation and opening the gates of heaven for us. Now the Risen Lord says to us, "Make your home in me as I make mine in you" (John 15:4).

As we say the *Our Father*, we share God the Father's joy at the resurrection of his beloved Son. The resurrection is the Father's response to the awful passion and crucifixion of Jesus. As he hung on the cross, the Gospel records, "The chief priests with their scribes and elders mocked him. 'He saved others,' they said, 'he cannot save himself. He is the king of Israel; let him come down from the cross now, and we will believe in him. He put his trust in God; now let God rescue him if he wants him. For he did say, "I am the Son of God"'" (Mathew 27:41–43). The resurrection shows just how much the Father "wanted him" because the resurrection is the fulfilment of the Father's plan for the salvation of the whole human race. As Jesus said, "God loved the world so much that he gave up his only Son, so that everyone who believes in him may not be lost but may have eternal life" (John 3:16).

The Guarantee of Our Eternal Life

The resurrection is the Father's guarantee to us that we will have eternal life because he has given us the same Holy Spirit which raised Jesus from the dead. St Paul says to us, "If the Spirit of him who raised up Jesus Christ from the dead is living in you, then he who raised up Jesus Christ from the dead will give life to your mortal bodies through his Spirit living in you" (Romans 8:11). What a wonderful promise! We have within us, even now in this world, the Spirit who raised Jesus from the dead. And, when we come to die, even though we will be buried, as Jesus was, the Spirit living within us will raise us up to eternal life with God. In the presence of the Spirit of God who is, as we say in the Creed, "the Lord, the giver of life", there can be no eternal death, only eternal life.

Blessed is She Who Believed

As we say our *Hail Marys*, we enter into Mary's joy at the resurrection of her Son. She lived through the terrible desolation and pain of her Son's passion and death. The prophecy of Simeon, when she presented the baby Jesus in the Temple, "a sword will pierce your own soul too" (Luke 2:35), has been fulfilled. But her unwavering faith in God's promise has now been rewarded. She can sing again her *Magnificat*: "My soul proclaims the greatness of the Lord and my spirit exults in God my saviour" (Luke 1:46–47). She now experiences that greatness of God's mighty love and power as her Son rises gloriously from the grave.

Jesus was conceived in Mary's womb through the power of the Holy Spirit. It is now through the power of that same Holy Spirit that Jesus is raised into the life of the resurrection. In making "our home" in the Risen Lord, we remember the love and the fellowship of the Holy Spirit. We give praise to the Holy Trinity as we say, *Glory be to the Father and to the Son and to the Holy Spirit*.

Prayer of Intercession

O Mother of Perpetual Succour, obtain for us the grace to make our home in this Mystery of your Son, our Lord Jesus Christ, as we meditate on the great mercy that the "Father of mercies" has shown to us.

The Second Glorious Mystery

The Ascension of Jesus into Heaven

After his resurrection Jesus appeared to his disciples on a number of occasions. He ate and drank with them; he gave them further teaching on the Kingdom of God; he promised that they would receive power when the Holy Spirit came. But he had to leave them. St Luke relates: "Then he took them out as far as the outskirts of Bethany, and lifting up his hands he blessed them. Now as he blessed them, he withdrew from them and was carried up into heaven. They worshipped him and went back to Jerusalem full of joy; and they were continually in the Temple praising God" (Luke 24:50–53).

What was it about the ascension of their Lord that filled them with joy instead of sadness at his leaving them? Their experience of the Risen Lord made it possible for them to understand in a new way what he meant when he said, "I am going away, and shall return. If you loved me you would have been glad to know that I am going to the Father, for the Father is greater than I" (John 14:28).

The disciples loved Jesus and so they were "full of joy" because Jesus was now with the Father. And they remembered what he said on the night before he suffered: "I am going now to prepare a place for you, and after I have gone and prepared you a place, I shall return to take you with me; so that where I am you may be too" (John 14:2–3). On that night they said, "Lord, we do not know where you are going, so how can we know the way?" (John 14:5). Now they know that Jesus is the way. And they believe that Jesus will return to take them to the Father's house. The angel had said to them as they watched Jesus ascend into heaven, "Jesus who has been taken up from you into heaven, this same Jesus will come back in the same way as you have seen him go there" (Acts 1:11).

I Am With You Always

Even though Jesus was leaving them, he was at the same time assuring them that he would be with them always. St Matthew tells us that, at the last meeting Jesus had with the disciples, he said to them: "All authority in heaven and earth has been given to me. Go, therefore, make disciples of all nations; baptise them in the name of the Father and of the Son and of the Holy Spirit, and teach them to observe all the commands I gave to you. And look, I am with you always; yes, to the end of time" (Matthew 28:18–20). Jesus' ascension is not his withdrawal into some different cosmos: it is his return to the "right hand of the Father", the Creator of all that is.

Jesus is closer to the disciples in his ascension than he was when walking the roads of Galilee with them. That is why the disciples are full of joy: they know and experience that he is closer to them now, in his physical absence, than when he was visibly present with them. He has become the centre of their lives.

Like those first Apostles, we too can be full of joy at Jesus' ascension because we too believe that now, at the right hand of God the Father, Jesus is closer to us than ever before. In fact, he says to us: "If anyone loves me he will keep my word and my Father will love him and we shall come to him and make our home with him" (John 14:23).

God Makes His Home in Us

As we "make our home" in the mystery of Christ's ascension into heaven, God the Father and Jesus come to make their home in us. What an exchange! In praying this mystery of the Rosary we will be filled with joy if we open our hearts in gratitude, humility and repentance for all our sins, and welcome the indwelling of the Holy Trinity at the core of our being.

While praying the *Our Father* we want to share in the Father's joy. He had sent Jesus into this world to redeem us. Having carried out his mission of love, Jesus returns to take his place at the right hand of his Father. If, as Jesus said, "there is joy in heaven over one sinner doing penance", there must have been immense joy in heaven as Jesus, having "saved his people from their sins" (Matthew 1:21), returns to his Father's house. That is the joy that filled the Apostles after Jesus' ascension and that is the joy the Father wants us to have in our hearts as we pray to him and "make our home" in this Mystery of his Son.

His Reign Will Have No End

Our *Hail Mary*s should also be full of joy as we open our hearts in love and confidence to share the joy that was in Mary's heart as her Son was taken up into heaven. At the annunciation, the Archangel Gabriel had told her, "He will be great and will be called Son of the Most High. The Lord God will give him the throne of his ancestor David; he will rule over the House of Jacob for ever and his reign will have no end" (Luke 1:32–33). Mary never doubted that promise of God, even at the foot of the cross. Now she witnesses it being fulfilled, as her Son, flesh of her flesh, takes his place at the right hand of the Most High. Jesus, in our very humanity, is at the right hand of the Father of Mercies. When Mary says to him on our behalf, "They have no wine," Jesus will never refuse her request. She is always his mother and Our Mother of Perpetual Succour.

Prayer of Intercession

O Mother of Perpetual Succour, obtain for us the grace to make our home in this Mystery of your Son, our Lord Jesus Christ, as we meditate on the great mercy that the "Father of mercies" has shown to us.

The Third Glorious Mystery
The Descent of the Holy Spirit

God the Father's great promise to his people in the Old Covenant was: "I will pour out my Spirit on all mankind" (Joel 2:28). It is through Our Lord Jesus Christ that the Father fulfils his promise. Jesus spoke to his disciples many times about the "gift of God" which is the Spirit. He said to them: "It is for your own good that I am going because unless I go, the Advocate will not come to you; but if I do go I will send him to you" (John 16:7).

Just before he ascended into heaven, Jesus told them to wait for what the Father had promised. "It is what you have heard me speak about. John baptised with water but you, not many days from now, will be baptised with the Holy Spirit" (Acts 1:4–5).

Waiting with Mary

The disciples waited, we are told, "in continuous prayer, together with several women, including Mary the mother of Jesus, and his brothers" (Acts 1:14). As they waited and prayed, the Father's promise was fulfilled. The Holy Spirit was poured out. This is the graphic description that we find in the Acts of the Apostles: "They heard what sounded like a powerful wind from heaven, the noise filled the entire house in which they were sitting, and something appeared to them that seemed like tongues of fire; these separated and came to rest on the head of each of them. They were all filled with the Holy Spirit" (Acts 2:2–4). The same Holy Spirit who came on Mary in Nazareth now comes on the disciples as they are united with her in prayer.

The Birth of the Church

The outpouring of the Holy Spirit was the fulfilment of God the Father's promise and, at the same time, the gift through which Jesus established his Church.

The Church was born on that first Pentecost Sunday when the Holy Spirit came and filled the disciples, as Jesus had promised. The Spirit wasn't given just for themselves. Jesus had given them the command: "Go, therefore, make disciples of all nations; baptise them in the name of the Father, the Son and the Holy Spirit, and teach them to observe all the commands I gave you. And know that I am with you always; yes, to the end of time" (Matthew 28:19–20). The disciples, in obedience to the Lord's command, "went out to the whole world to preach the Gospel" (Mark 16:20). We are disciples today because Christ continues to fulfil his promise and fills us with the Holy Spirit.

"Making our home" in this mystery of Christ pouring out his Spirit on the disciples enables us to discover our true identity as the Church of Christ, his Mystical Body in the world. When the Holy Spirit came on Mary at the annunciation in Nazareth, the Son of God became man in her womb. Now, when that same Holy Spirit comes upon the disciples, they become the mystical Body of Christ in the world.

God the Father's Promise is Fulfilled

It is because God the Father has fulfilled his promise to pour out the Holy Spirit through the death and resurrection of Christ that we are now the members of Christ's Mystical Body, members of the

Church, temples of the Holy Spirit. We pray the *Our Father* in this decade of the Rosary with the grateful awareness that the Father has fulfilled his promise to us and filled us with the Holy Spirit.

When we pray our ten *Hail Marys* in this decade, we remember the words that Elizabeth spoke to Mary when she greeted her: "Blessed is the fruit of your womb" (Luke 1:42). Mary saw how blessed indeed was the fruit of her womb as the Holy Spirit came on the disciples on that first Pentecost Sunday. Just as when the Holy Spirit caused the Incarnation of her Son Jesus in her womb, Jesus now sends that same Holy Spirit into his disciples and his Mystical Body, the Church, is born into this world.

In that moment of the birth of her Son's Mystical Body, through the coming of the Holy Spirit, Mary surely understood the full significance of the final words Jesus spoke to her from the cross: "Woman, this is your son" (John 19:26). Mary realised that she had been given, by the word of God spoken by her Son, a new motherhood. She is the Mother of the Church of Christ which is her Son's Mystical Body in the world.

With this awareness of all that the Father has done for us through Jesus and through the gift of the Holy Spirit, we say with even greater gratitude, *Glory be to the Father and to the Son and to the Holy Spirit.*

Prayer of Intercession

O Mother of Perpetual Succour, obtain for us the grace to make our home in this Mystery of your Son, our Lord Jesus Christ, as we meditate on the great mercy that the "Father of mercies" has shown to us.

The Fourth Glorious Mystery
The Assumption of Our Lady into Heaven

Our reflections on the mysteries of Christ in the Rosary began with the Annunciation, when the archangel Gabriel was sent by God to ask Mary to become the mother of God the Son, Our Lord Jesus Christ.

Now, as we come to the last two mysteries, Mary is once again at the centre of our reflection. We believe that after her death Mary was assumed, body and soul, into heaven, where her Son Jesus was already seated at the right hand of the Father.

This is a beautiful mystery to ponder. It is the mystery of the Father's grateful thanks to Mary for consenting to collaborate with him in the work of our redemption. When God asked her to become the mother of his Son, Mary wholeheartedly said her "Yes". The Assumption is also the mystery of the filial love of her Son Jesus, who receives his mother, after her death, into heaven where he, in the flesh and blood he received from her, now reigns as Lord.

"All Generations Will Call Me Blessed"

Mary foretold that "All generations will call me blessed" (Luke 1:48). When Mary died, her own generation, those who accepted her Son Jesus as their Lord and Saviour, would have been calling her blessed. St Luke would not have recorded Mary's prophecy about all generations calling her blessed if his own generation hadn't already begun to call her blessed.

The death of Mary is not recorded in the New Testament. We have no accounts of how she died or what happened after her death. Nor was there ever any claim on the part of any city or church to have the tomb of Mary. Within the faith of the Church there developed the conviction that Mary was assumed body and soul into heaven.

From the sixth century onward this conviction of faith was strong in the universal Church, in both the East and the West.

Church's Faith in the Assumption Inspired by the Holy Spirit

Like her Son Jesus, Mary underwent death. And just as death could not hold the body of Christ in its grasp, so too, through the power of the Risen Christ, death could not hold the body of his Mother in its grasp. Mary was assumed into heaven.

The Church believes that its faith in the Assumption of Our Lady was aroused and sustained over the centuries by the Holy Spirit. As the Church pondered the mystery of Mary's divine motherhood it began to see that the sinless Mother of Jesus, the risen Lord, was already sharing in his victory over sin and death. Christ's human, risen and glorified body was born of Mary. He was flesh of her flesh. Could Christ allow the body of his sinless Mother, who gave birth to his own victorious and risen body, to lie in the corruption of the grave? Would Christ, who will share his resurrection with all his brothers and sisters at the end of time, not anticipate this general resurrection and receive his Mother, body and soul, into heaven? The instinct of Catholic faith was that he could and that he did.

The Sign of Sure Hope

In the Preface of the Mass of the Assumption, the Church presents Mary's Assumption as a sure sign of hope for us all:

> Today the Virgin Mother of God was assumed into heaven as the beginning and image of your Church's coming to perfection and a sign of sure hope and comfort to your pilgrim people; rightly you would not allow her to see the corruption of the tomb since from her own body she marvellously brought forth your incarnate Son, the Author of life.

In Mary's Assumption we see our own eternal destiny. Just as Mary is now body and soul in heaven, so we too, at the resurrection of the dead on the Last Day, will be like Mary in our resurrected bodies. This is surely a source of great hope for us as we make our journey through this life.

Because Mary, in body and soul, is now with Christ in heaven she can relate to each of her children on earth in an individual and personal way. In the new creation, where God is all in all, Mary can now have a personal relationship with all the members of Christ's body on earth, with all the members of the Church. Mary is in a personal relationship with you when you speak to her and say her Rosary. She knows your name and comes to your help. She is truly Our Mother of Perpetual Succour.

The Immaculate Virgin Mary

We remember, as we say the *Our Father,* that it was the Father who chose Mary to be the Mother of his Son. It was the Father who gave Mary the grace of her Immaculate Conception and was the first to call her "full of grace"! Mary was born into this world free from all sin through the foreseen merits of her Son's redemptive death and resurrection. She lived her whole life in communion with God, so that she could be the worthy mother of the Son of God. The Father rejoices now that the Mother of his Son is taking her place, body and soul, in his house, in heaven.

As we say our *Hail Mary*s we remember that the Mary to whom we are speaking is body and soul in heaven. As our heavenly Mother, she is very close to us on earth. She is now present as mother to each of us in the mystery of Christ, the mystery of the Church. She hears our prayers and listens to our requests, especially when we pray, *Holy Mary, Mother of God, pray for us sinners.*

We conclude this decade remembering especially the presence and the work of the Holy Spirit in the life and mission of our Mother Mary and we say with reverence, *Glory be to the Father and to the Son and to the Holy Spirit.*

Prayer of Intercession

O Mother of Perpetual Succour, obtain for us the grace to make our home in this Mystery of your Son, our Lord Jesus Christ, as we meditate on the great mercy that the "Father of mercies" has shown to us.

The Fifth Glorious Mystery
The Crowning of Our Lady in Heaven

Mary, the Mother of Christ, the King of heaven and earth, is honoured in the Church as the Queen of heaven and earth. St Alphonsus de' Liguori begins his great work *The Glories of Mary* by stating: "As the glorious Virgin Mary has been raised to the dignity of Mother of the King of Kings, it is not without reason that the Church honours her, and wishes her to be honoured by all, with the glorious title of Queen."[35]

For centuries the faithful have meditated on this final Mystery of the Rosary, the Crowning of Our Lady in heaven. And, indeed, the faithful, for centuries, have concluded the Rosary by saying the *Salve Regina*, the beautiful *Hail Holy Queen, Mother of Mercy* prayer to Our Lady. With a sure instinct of faith, the Catholic faithful believed that the Lord Jesus, having assumed his Mother, body and soul, into heaven, seated her at 'his right hand' and crowned her Queen. Throughout the whole of Christian history Mary has been acknowledged as Queen. The Second Vatican Council affirmed this faith and devotion of the Catholic people:

> The immaculate Virgin, preserved free from all stain of original sin, was taken up body and soul into heavenly glory, when her earthly life was over, and exalted by the Lord as Queen over all things, that she might be the more fully conformed to her Son, the Lord of lords (see Apocalypse 19:16) and conqueror of sin and death.[36]

Feast of the Queenship of Mary

We honour and acknowledge Mary as Queen because we honour and worship Jesus her Son as King. Writing about the feast of the Queenship of Mary, which Pope Pius XII instituted in 1954, after he had defined the dogma of the Assumption, Blessed Pope Paul VI wrote:

> The solemnity of the Assumption is prolonged in the celebration of the Queenship of the Blessed Virgin Mary, which occurs seven days later. On this day we contemplate her who, seated beside the King of Ages, shines forth as Queen and intercedes as Mother.

Mary was crowned Queen of Heaven not to dominate but to serve, not to remain aloof from God's people but to be their Mother of Perpetual Succour.

The Council refers to that ancient prayer that has come down to us from those earliest times: "We fly to thy protection, O Holy Mother of God, despise not our petitions in our necessities, but deliver us from all danger, O ever glorious and Blessed Virgin." The Greek version of this ancient prayer dates from the beginning of the third century. Since this prayer had already been written down – and writing was not all that common in those days – the Christians of Alexandria in Egypt, where the prayer was first committed to writing, could have been saying that prayer from as early as the second century. Cardinal Shönborn, commenting on this ancient prayer, writes, "The oldest versions of this prayer, written on papyrus, have a peculiar feature that is quite beautiful. They do not begin with 'We fly to thy patronage' but rather 'we fly to thy mercy, O Mother of God'." As we salute Mary in the *Hail Holy Queen,* we call her Mother of Mercy.

It is surely significant that at this very early stage in the development of the Church, only decades after the death of St John the Evangelist, Christians were turning to Our Lady and asking for her powerful intercession. In the Catholic Church we have always believed that it is the Holy Spirit who inspires this confidence in Mary's intercession, which is the secret of all devotion to Mary.

The Generation that Calls Mary Blessed

We began our reflections on the mysteries of the Rosary with the Annunciation, when Our Lady identified herself as "the handmaid of the Lord" (Luke 1:38) and when she said to Elizabeth, "He has looked upon his lowly handmaid" (Luke 1:48). In her serene self-acceptance she was able to rejoice in what God was doing in her: "From this day forward all generations will call me blessed, for the Lord has done great things for me" (Luke 1:48–49). We rejoice today that we belong to the generation that calls her blessed. We rejoice that Mary, the "humble handmaid of the Lord", is Queen of heaven and earth and our Mother of Perpetual Succour. As St Pope John Paul II wrote: "In her new motherhood in the Spirit, Mary embraces each and every one *in* the Church, and she embraces each and every one *through* the Church."[39]

Our Great Trinitarian Devotion

As we pray the *Our Father* we keep in mind the truth that our salvation is the manifestation of God the Father's great love for us. We also keep in mind that the Father reconciled us to himself through Our Lord Jesus Christ who was born of the Virgin Mary by the power of the Holy Spirit. That is why I said at the very beginning of this book that the Rosary is our greatest Trinitarian prayer. In every mystery we see the presence and the love of the three divine persons, Father, Son and Holy Spirit. The mysteries of Christ are manifestations of the Father's love: "God loved the world so much that he gave his only Son, so that those who believe in him may not be lost but may have eternal life" (John 3:16).

While we pray the *Hail Mary*s we remember that Mary our Mother, in being crowned Queen of heaven and earth, loves each one of us as her son or daughter and that she is interceding for us with her Son. In her glorified body in heaven we gaze on what our human bodies will become when we enter "the Father's house". As our Queen and Mother, Mary now fills us with great trust and confidence in God. As the Second Vatican Council said:

> The Mother of Jesus, in the glory which she possesses in body and soul in heaven, is the image and the beginning of the Church as it is to be perfected in the world to come. Likewise she shines forth on earth, until the day of the Lord shall come (cf. 2 Peter 3:10), as a sign of certain hope and comfort to the pilgrim People of God.[40]

We acknowledge Our Lady as that "sign of certain hope" when we pray, "Hail Holy Queen, Mother of Mercy, hail our life, our sweetness and our hope." We honour Our Lady as Queen of heaven and earth and we also honour her as Our Mother of Perpetual Succour.

Prayer of Intercession

O Mother of Perpetual Succour, obtain for us the grace to make our home in this Mystery of your Son, our Lord Jesus Christ, as we meditate on the great mercy that the "Father of mercies" has shown to us.

Notes

[1] Blessed Paul VI, *To Honour Mary*, 47

[2] Pope Francis, *Misericordiae Vultus: Bull of Indiction of the Extraordinary Jubilee Year of Mercy*, 1

[3] *Sayings of Cardinal Newman* (London: Burns Oates, c.1890/2004), p. 44

[4] Pope Benedict XVI, *God is Love*, para 1

[5] Pope Francis, *Misericordiae Vultus: Bull of Indiction of the Extraordinary Jubilee Year of Mercy*, 1

[6] 3rd Eucharistic Prayer

[7] Pope Benedict XVI, *The Infancy Narratives: Jesus of Nazareth* (London: Bloomsbury, 2012), p. 124

[8] Pope Benedict XVI, *Jesus of Nazareth: From the Baptism in the Jordan to the Transfiguration* (London: Bloomsbury, 2007), p. 18

[9] Raymond E. Brown, *The Gospel According to John*, Anchor Bible 29 (Garden City, NY: Doubleday, 1966), 1:99

[10] Brant Pitre, *Jesus the Bridegroom: The Greatest Love Story Ever Told* (New York: Image, 2014), p. 45

[11] Pope Francis, *Misericordiae Vultus: Bull of Indiction of the Extraordinary Jubilee Year of Mercy*, 1

[12] St Pope John Paul II, *Mission of the Redeemer*, 18

[13] Pope Benedict XVI, *God is Love*, para 1

[14] Constitution on the Church in Modern World, 22

[15] St Pope John Paul II, *Redeemer of Man*, 10

[16] Pope Benedict XVI, *Jesus of Nazareth: From the Baptism in the Jordan to the Transfiguration* (London: Bloomsbury, 2007), p. 311

[17] Ibid., p. 313

[18] St Pope John Paul II, *Encyclical on the Eucharist*, 11

[19] St Alphonsus de' Liguori, *The Holy Eucharist* (Centenary Edition, 1887), p. 239

[20] 2nd Eucharistic Prayer

[21] Pope Francis, *Laudato si'*, p. 236

[22] Cited in Raniero Cantalamessa, *The Eucharist* (Collegeville, MN: Liturgical Press, 1993), p. 39

[23] Pope Benedict XVI, *Jesus of Nazareth: From the Baptism in the Jordan to the Transfiguration* (London: Bloomsbury, 2007), p. 18

[24] Pope Benedict XVI, *Jesus of Nazareth, Part 2* (London: Catholic Truth Society, 2011), p. 1986

[25] Ibid., p. 198

[26] Brant Pitre, *Jesus the Bridegroom: The Greatest Love Story Ever Told* (New York: Image, 2014), p. 104

[27] St Alphonsus de' Liguori, *The Stations of the Cross* (London: Catholic Truth Society, 2015), p. 11

[28] Ibid., 13

[29] Pope Benedict XVI, *Jesus of Nazareth, Part 2* (London: Catholic Truth Society, 2011), p. 231

[30] *Constitution on the Sacred Liturgy*, para 5

[31] Pope Benedict XVI, *Jesus of Nazareth, Part 2* (London: Catholic Truth Society, 2011), p. 221

[32] Alphonsus de' Liguori, *Classics of Western Spirituality* (New York: Paulists, 1999), p. 26

[33] Ibid.

[34] Pope Francis, *Misericordiae Vultus: Bull of Indiction of the Extraordinary Jubilee Year of Mercy*, 1

[35] St Alphonsus de' Liguori, *The Glories of Mary*

[36] Constitution on the Church in the Modern World, 59

[37] Blessed Paul VI, *To Honour Mary*, 6

[38] Christoph Cardinal Shönborn, *We Have Found Mercy* (San Francisco: Ignatius Press, 2012), p. 119

[39] St Pope John Paul II, *Mother of the Redeemer*, 47

[40] Constitution on the Church in the Modern World, 68